The Essence of Motherhood

THE UPS AND DOWNS OF BEING A MOM

RADHIKA JINDAL

For all moms and moms-to-be

© **Radhika Jindal 2022**

All rights reserved

All rights reserved by author. No part of this publication may be reproduced, stored in a retrieval system or transmitted in any form or by any means, electronic, mechanical, photocopying, recording or otherwise, without the prior permission of the author.

Although every precaution has been taken to verify the accuracy of the information contained herein, the author and publisher assume no responsibility for any errors or omissions. No liability is assumed for damages that may result from the use of information contained within.

First Published in January 2022

ISBN: 978-93-5472-796-2

BLUEROSE PUBLISHERS
www.bluerosepublishers.com
info@bluerosepublishers.com
+91 8882 898 898

Cover Design:
Geetika Kandari

Typographic Design:
Pooja Sharma

Distributed by: BlueRose, Amazon, Flipkart

Dedication

Dedicated to all "Parents-to-be"!

About The Author

Born into a conservative family in Hisar, Haryana, Radhika was very modest and introspective as she was growing up. The birth of her daughter changed everything - she suddenly found her purpose in life and felt like she was reborn as a new person. Much more confident than ever before, she realized there was so much she could do in life. To understand this new perspective better, she started attending workshop sessions by various coaches and eventually started sharing her experiences via her blog ((www.radhikadiary.com) in which she speaks about books, motherhood, and self-love. She stays in a joint family with her in-laws, husband, and her princess, Divyanshi. When she's not writing or working, she loves reading, cooking, and explore new places. She loves socializing with like-minded people.

Instagram: radhika0001
Facebook: radhikadiary
Blog: www.radhikadiary.com

Praise For The Book

Isn't it great to read the real-life experiences of a mother who shares her journey from pregnancy to motherhood? If you are in the process of having a baby or planning a baby, THE ESSENCE OF MOTHERHOOD is one of those valuable books that can give you a plethora of information about pregnancy and motherhood. Through this book, Radhika has explained very well about the three trimesters of the beautiful journey of bringing a new life to the world.

Being pregnant completely changes a woman's life, routine, and her priorities. Radhika has beautifully explained all the challenges faced by a mother pre- and post-delivery, how she can take care of herself in her postpartum time, the support that she needs from her family members; every aspect of the motherhood journey has been highlighted in this book. I really appreciate the way she has prepared a checklist of things that every mother or her family should keep a note of before getting her admitted for delivery.

I wish I had a book like this during my pregnancies. When to start your fitness regime as your body goes out of shape after delivering the baby? How having a new baby around the house can bring happiness to your life? You will get answers to these and many more such questions.

I have known Radhika for quite a while now and she is doing a wonderful job as a blogger where she reviews books of new authors. She is extremely talented. Best wishes to her for her new venture.

SEEMA DHALL

Author of "Walking With Your Child"

I love how all the topics are covered in this book for expecting mothers and new mothers.

She has quite honestly given out a few of her life examples of how she faced few issues pre- and post-delivery. One that touched my heart is post-pregnancy depression! Yes, this is something that most of us won't talk about. Glad that this is added in the book. Love the suggestions that come out from her own experiences.

A must read for someone who wants to get some information about pregnancy and newborn without much technical and hard issues. Well written and covered what's more important in a composed way.

Sadvika Kylash

Author of "Motherhood Talks"

Blogger @ https://momlifeandlifestyle.com/

When you are thinking about having a baby, you want some guidance, wisdom and calm narration with full clarity that is put together in the form of a book by the proficient person. I appreciated the clearly phrased and precisely detailed chapters; new moms are given nutritional, psychological, and fitness advice with plenty of confident encouragement. The book also acknowledges various difficulties that occur at every stage and represents diversity in the information. If you are a first-time mom, definitely check out this book.

Dr Priyadarshinia

Author of the journal "Invoking joy within"

"The Essence of Motherhood" is a treasure of advises and guidance from a mother to a mother-to-be. Throughout this book, the author had highlighted the key events during and after pregnancy which is essential to be taken care of. She has beautifully brought out the importance of Garb Sanskar and the role of family member during pregnancy and after child birth. A MUST READ for every couple who are planning for pregnancy.

- Dr. Abinaya Vijayakumar

Motherhood Empowerment Coach and Author of International No. 1 BestSeller "OMG! I AM A MOM NOW"

An expert's advice or a guided support system is very important to any expectant mother to experience a healthy pregnancy. At the same time, strong emotional support is equally important. Often for that purpose, she longs for a very dear friend, a confidante, who has already walked her path, can solve all her doubts, and guide her towards facing the challenges in a realistic way.

While reading the book "Essence of Motherhood" written by Radhika Jindal, I honestly felt that I was sitting beside a very close friend of mine and listening to her pregnancy journey. In that sense, I feel this book will definitely act like a very good friend for any expectant mother, throughout her pregnancy, the birth, and beyond!

Worries in pregnancy arise due to the misinformation, myths, wrong beliefs, or lack of knowledge, "Essence of Motherhood" provides an overview of pretty much everything an expectant mother would want to know to overcome those unwanted worries. It is written in a very engaging manner, dotted with real-life experiences, expert interviews, and poetry, making this book unique and beautiful.

Dr Shruthi M S (Author of the book "Blooming Beyond Pain")

If you wish to cherish and enjoy your golden nine months and transform them into the most beautiful and incredible memories of your life, this book is for you!

Komal Agarwal (Mother & Environment Specialist)

Foreword

"The Essence of Motherhood" is meant for every expecting mom to pick up and get answers to never-ending questions that arise during her journey of pregnancy and one year after that. The book is specifically helpful for the first-time mom who is surrounded by confusion and who gets relentless advice from other moms and relations.

Pregnancy and motherhood are unique experiences for every mom, yet similar at various levels. Few suggestions from others can help, but ignorance makes this journey hard. A book like this can help expecting or new moms to get restful nights with a comfort in the knowledge that she knows what can be expected and how to handle each step as it comes.

Many experts have been consulted for this book, making it authentic and trustworthy. I like the healthy diet suggestions provided for every trimester. The chapter on Garbh Sanskar is my personal favourite as it presents meditation exercises that can help an expecting mother to relax.

Every new or expecting mom will find some relevant information throughout this book for her wellness and her child's healthy growth.

I congratulate Radhika Jindal and wish her all the best for her future endeavors.

Warm regards

Vandana Sehgal (Author | Holistic Wellness Coach | Book Writing Coach)

Acknowledgement

Writing a book is not easy. Especially when there is an active child constantly needing your attention. I am so grateful to the many people in my life who have all come together to make this possible for me. This book has been a dream of mine for many years.

Thanks to my Nani ji, Geeta Devi, who had written a book on Marwadi wedding sangeet. It is from her that I got the inspiration to write a book.

Both my moms, that is my mother, Mamta Aggarwal, and mother-in-law, Kanta Jindal — thank you for being so supportive throughout my pregnancy, and teaching me many of the things I know today about bringing up a baby.

I am extremely grateful to both my father, Mr. Manoj Aggarwal, and my father-in-law, Mr. KCJ Jindal, for showing faith in me.

If I have to thank anyone in the word after my parents and in-laws then it's my husband, Kapil Jindal who supported me continuously by showing a great faith in me. He was patient, encouraging and supportive all through the writing process.

I thank my sister-in-laws, Komal Agarwal and Khushboo Kaur, my brother-in-laws, Mayank Agarwal and Ajeet Singh, my brother Harsh and sister-in-law Sneha, and my cousins, for always being there for me.

I am extremely grateful to my mentors — Amrita Mitroo (book coach and a 5-star rated author), Ms Kailash Jayani (life skill coach), Vandana Sehgal (author and holistic coach), Deepak (author) — for all the support, advice and encouragement.

I thank the wonderful contributors of the book for taking time out to write their thoughts — Shweta, Dr. Charu, Dr. Abinnaya, Dr. Shilpi, Priyanka, Monali, and Rommal for being so kind and for being a part of this book.

I am grateful to all the team members of the book — Savita, Dr Ms Shruthi, Komal Agarwal, Priyadarshini, and Mrs. Seema Dhall.

My heartfelt thanks to the editor, Rhinusmita, who made my dream come true. I felt so connected with her from the first day we spoke. She is a mother of 3 kids herself and that's what made us to relate with each other's feelings so well.

I would like to give thanks to the Blogchatter team. I published my short ebook on their website for a short period of time. The good response made me continue writing and sharing my feelings with other moms via this book.

And finally, the best one for the last, I thank my dearest, adorable princess, Divanshi, for giving me hope, for giving me this beautiful gift of motherhood, and for all the love I never realized I had in me before.

Thanks to two little munchkins Divyam and the new born.

Preface

How and why was this book written

Despite being healthy and financially secure, I wasn't satisfied with the life I was living. Even while I went through motions of life, which appeared very happy and full to anyone looking in, there was something that wouldn't let me sleep, a missing link somewhere. When I finally went to sleep, it would not be sound, and I always woke up tired. There seemed to be no excitement, no purpose in life. I felt the lack of something I couldn't identify, something my soul needed.

One day, when I sat down to meditate, I had a conversation with God and tried asking what are the plans for me? I started questioning myself. These meditation sessions opened my inner self. I surrendered myself to the universe.

Soon after this, I came across a workshop called "**Know Your Why**". It was being conducted by Infinite Kailash Sir, leadership and biz growth expert (Founder and Chairman of MindXL). I hesitated a bit, just a bit, before I went ahead. It was probably the best thing I did in a long time. That day changed my life completely, and I figured out what my "*why*" is. At home, I brainstormed a lot of things with my husband who always listens to me patiently and gives me the bestest advice. Gradually, I started writing blogs and writing book reviews. To my surprise, my blog became almost an instant hit. The recognition and appreciation I got for my work from authors and my readers satisfied and fulfilled my life in so many ways. As I continued my journey, I learnt a lot and my self-confidence was boosted. I regained the essence of life that I was missing.

I always have a number of thoughts going through my mind. Something is always cooking. I finally took pen and paper to give shape to my thoughts. As I kept writing, I realized that I have so many ideas and thoughts to share with others. There are many new moms who are at the same stage where I was and seeking advice from others. I know how it feels when you face everything in life for the first time and you're seeking guidance. Though experience is the best teacher, there are quite a few things that help us in preparing ourselves a little in advance.

My primary motive behind writing this book is to help expectant moms and let them know pregnancy is a beautiful journey. Pregnancy is just the first step; the actual ride of a mother begins once "the baby is out". The entire period of pregnancy is something to be savoured, a period of learning and preparation as you await the arrival of the tiny person who will change your life forever. I wanted to share my experiences and that of other mothers and experts to help many new moms or moms-to-be. Hope you enjoy the book!

Introduction

Messy Motherhood

"You're also born again along with the baby." – Radhika

Do you think motherhood is messy, along with messy houses, messy rooms, and messy clothes? If your answer is yes! Then yes! It is. It's messy and beautiful. The mess is good when it is by your own kids. You can never have a clean house with a newborn and a toddler at home. Be proud. Feel proud to have a kid at home. My message here's not to scare you but to give you the vibes of this beautiful mess. If you are already in that stage, you can totally relate to what I'm trying to convey.

Congratulations if you're already on the journey. Best of luck to those who're trying to conceive. You would sense a feeling of excitement and nervousness the moment you see those two red lines after you take the tests. I remember the day when I took the pregnancy test and told my husband about it. We were both nervous and excited at the same time. Those two lines completely changed our life and this was our first child. There were so many doubts like - What to do now? What's next? Whom to contact? My mind was full of questions like weight gain, diet plans, delivery mode, how to find a good gynaecologist, prenatal classes, and what not!?

A new life will be blooming soon in the womb, so we needed to be prepared and yet be relaxed. Many of you may be in the same situation as I was some years back. I have written this book after a lot of research, personal experience, and with advice from experts and the experiences of moms from different parts of the world so that it comes as a total package with advice, tips and tricks for almost every kind of situation you and your partner may face in motherhood. Each chapter has some key takeaways and is written in a friendly voice. You can expect a lot of professional advice like from a nutritionist, dentist, mental health blogger, obstetrician, and experienced mothers that will help you to make your pregnancy smooth.

A little about the book: What to expect from this book when you are expecting?

The book is divided into two sections:

Healthy Pregnancy: Pregnancy is divided into three phases called the three trimesters and I have tried to cover all the unique issues and events that occur in each trimester, answering the questions that most mothers or to-be-mothers have. A few topics include healthy diet plans and exercise, maintaining self-love, garbh sanskar, packing your hospital bag, and how prepare yourself for the D-day.

Cherish the Motherhood: At the end of nine months, you are able to hold your baby in your hands and see him or her for the first time. You are now officially a 'Mother'! The second part of my book is about the so-called official motherhood stage once the baby is delivered. How can you take care of yourself in the postpartum period? How has your role as a mother changed now? How does your relationship with your spouse change? How can you keep yourself happy? In this section, I have tried to answer all kinds of parenting questions you may have.

I am just one of you who likes to help others and I hope this book would be a valuable guide for the expecting mothers and dads-to-be. The book will help you in having a positive mindset towards pregnancy. It'll also give you a glimpse of what you can expect during and after the pregnancy phase. Motherhood is a beautiful journey but not a destination. This book will help you through this journey like a friend, a guide, and sometimes like a mother or mother-in-law.

Contents

Part 1 Healthy Pregnancy 1

Chapter 1: A Beautiful Surprise 2

Chapter 2: The Three Trimesters: Your Health, Exercise And Diet Plans 11

Chapter 3: Garbh Sanskar 39

Chapter 4: In-Laws And The Father-To-Be 48

Chapter 5: Give A Gift To Yourself - Mental, Physical, Social, And Spiritual Happiness 56

Chapter 6: Hospital Bag Checklist 65

Chapter 7: Finally, The Day Arrives: Natural Birth Or C-Section? 69

Chapter 8: Conclusion - The Beautiful New Journey Ahead 76

Part 2 Cherish The Motherhood 84

Chapter 9: Postpartum Blues: How To Handle Postpartum Depression And The Weight Challenge 85

Chapter 10: Lessons Learned In My Motherhood Journey 99

Chapter 11: Magical Motherhood 107

Chapter 12: Hats Off To Mothers 112

Chapter 13: Moms Sharing Their Experiences 118

Direct Dil Se For On My Daughter, Divanshi's 2nd B'day 125

References and Books Recommendations.......................... 127
Thank You Note.. 128

PART 1
Healthy Pregnancy

God could not be everywhere, and therefore he made mothers —Rudyard Kipling.

1

A Beautiful Surprise

"I trust that everything happens for a reason, even if we are not wise enough to see it." – Oprah Winfrey

Am I Pregnant?

Every day, approximately 67,385 babies are born in India. The pregnancy journey for each of the mothers of each of these babies is unique. Like your mother will say, every pregnancy is special, every pregnancy is different. Pregnancy is sometimes long awaited and at other times a complete surprise. In each case, however, the first indication that you may be pregnant is a missed or delayed period.

Each month, in the first half of the menstrual circle, one of the ovaries gets ready to release an egg. The uterus in turn gets ready to receive the fertilized egg. About 12-14 days into the cycle, the ovary releases the egg. This is called ovulation. It is while the egg is on its way from the ovary to the uterus that fertilization with a sperm takes place. So, suppose fertilization doesn't take place, the uterus sheds the lining that it had prepared and you get your period. On the other hand, if the egg gets fertilized, this will move into the uterus and get embedded. In this case, there will be no period. Have you missed your period this month?

Yes? Then hang on, don't panic, don't get super excited either. Take deep breaths, stay calm and wait for about 10 days.

If it's over 10 days, it's time to test and confirm the pregnancy. There are two ways in which you can do that: urine tests or blood tests.

Urine Tests

Before you visit the doctor, it is always best to use the pregnancy kit first if you have a doubt that you may be pregnant or if your period is delayed. There are many card kits available in medical stores. These are very low-cost and easy to use. The home kits are all urine tests measured by the levels of human chorionic gonadotropin (hCG). If you are reading this book, you are probably already familiar with the home testing kits.

Take the test preferably just after waking up in the morning. If two red lines are visible, that means your pregnancy is confirmed.

Did you see those two lines?

If yes, then congratulations!

If two lines are not visible, it doesn't mean you are not pregnant. Sometimes, there ae false negatives or it may be a bit early.

In both cases, it's time to

HCG Levels Chart

WEEKS FROM LAST MENSTRUAL PERIOD	APPROX. AMOUNT OF HCG (IN MIU/ML)
3 weeks	5 to 50
4 weeks	5 to 426
5 weeks	19 to 7,340
6 weeks	1,080 to 56,500
7-8 weeks	7,650 to 229,000
9-12 weeks	25,700 to 288,000
13-16 weeks	3,300 to 253,000
17-24 weeks (second trimester)	4,060 to 165,400
25 to term (third trimester)	3,640 to 117,000
After several days postpartum	Nonpregnant levels (<5)

visit your gynaecologist.

Blood Pregnancy Tests

Your doctor will probably advice a blood test to confirm your pregnancy. The weekly increase in the level of hCG in the blood usually follows a specific pattern. The levels of hCG might differ in both type of tests. A blood test is a more accurate test and will give the doctor more information.

Once it is confirmed, the doctor will advise you how to take care of yourself, probably prescribe vitamins, iron and folic acid, and tell you to avoid strenuous work. The doctor can ask you to take up an ultrasound test in the 6th-8th weeks when the baby's heartbeat appears.

So, Hey!! You have started taking the first steps of your motherhood journey!

What To Do If You Are Not Pregnant

I wish all the best for those couples who are trying to conceive. I hope God showers his love for them soon. A negative test is not the end of the world. For some, pregnancy happens quickly, for others it takes time. A lot has to do with the time of intercourse, your ovulation, and many other things.

The most important advice for a woman who wants to get pregnant is to get to know her body, specifically her menstrual cycle, says Dr. Mary Ellen Pavone, a reproductive endocrinologist and infertility specialist, and medical director of the in-vitro fertilization program at

Northwestern Medicine's Reproductive Endocrinology and Infertility division in Chicago.

The worst thing you can do is to stress yourself out by thinking too much about it. Like I said earlier, each pregnancy is different, each child comes in his or her own way.

Here are a few tips on how to conceive:

1. Track Your Menstrual Cycle frequency
2. Monitor the ovulation period
3. Make love during the fertile window
4. Try to maintain a healthy body weight
5. Take multivitamins under the consultation of your doctor
6. Eating healthy and be physically active
7. Avoid drinking/smoking

If it's been a long time that you have been trying to conceive, it is best to consult your doctor. Sometimes, there may be issues with either the husband or the wife that the doctor will be able to help with. Many of the women cannot conceive because of age, Polycystic Ovarian Disease (PCOD), or Endometriosis. These are three common causes. There are solutions for each and your doctor will be the best person to help you.

Women having PCOD need to maintain a healthy lifestyle, blood sugar levels and treating other PCOD symptoms with moderate weight and medications. They should take proper vitamins like folic acid, vitamin B6, vitamin B12, vitamin c, vitamin D, and vitamin D that may help in fertility. To get a healthy pregnancy, its mandatory to maintain a diet rich with fibre, protein, and healthy fats. If you have high blood sugar levels or type 2 diabetes, it's important to check your blood sugar levels with a home monitor every day.

Nowadays there are many other options like in vitro fertilization (IVF) for having a baby. So, there's always some solution.

Pregnancy Is Confirmed. Now What?

After the confirmation by the tests or by the doctor, you are now officially pregnant.

What's the next step?

It is observed that most couples don't reveal the pregnancy news in the first three months. However, close family like the parents on both sides (or would-be-grandparents), close friends are the first ones you feel like sharing the news with. As soon as you share the news, though, be prepared to get lots and lots of advice from all sides. Some of these advices may be completely contradictory to each other. Your mother may tell you to go for walks regularly while your mother-in-law may advice complete bed rest. Keep calm at all times and consult your doctor whenever there is any confusion.

Once you have calmed down from all the excitement, the first thing you can do is to download a *pregnancy app* to stay updated about the growth of your baby. You'll get to know about your unborn baby everyday like the height, the size, the weight, etc. There are various apps available and I would suggest going through Babycentre, Whattoexpect, Imumz, Mylo, and Hi Mommy. Choose the one that appeals to you most. The app, along with this book and other books, will help you plan out a healthy pregnancy.

In India, gender revelation is banned, and you will get to know whether your baby is a boy or a girl only after birth. This is very good as it becomes a big surprise. Do not try and ask the doctor or nurse to tell you the gender because this is an offence.

Keeping A Journal

These nine months are very precious because you and your baby are completely connected. Each day will be different and soon, once the child is born, you will probably forget the small, precious details. What I did to help preserve my memories is keep a journal. There are many ways in which

> How is the pregnancy due date calculated?
>
> Formula for calculating due dates:
>
> 1st day of last period + 7 days minus 3 months
>
> Example:
>
> 1st day of last period: May 15
>
> May 15 + 7 days = 22 May
>
> May 22 - 3 months = Feb 22

you can do this. You can use a diary, a scrapbook, or an online journal. Write down your feelings, add your ultrasound prints, share thoughts with your unborn child. Among online diaries, I have found Journey (https://journey.cloud/diary-journal-software) to be very friendly and you can attach audio or media files to it. Some moms to be start blogs in which they share their experience with many others. This too is something you can do, if you feel comfortable. For me, my pregnancy was a very personal and intimate experience and I preferred writing privately. Again, as I said, each pregnancy is different, each journey is different.

In the next chapter, I'll be discussing your self-care, diet plans and exercises for the three trimesters and what to expect in each trimester.

An interview with gynaecologist, Dr. Manju Gupta (MBBS, MS- Obstetrics & Gynaecology, Laparscopic Surgeon) with an experience of more than 15 years.

Author Radhika: What should both partner take care of before planning a baby?

Dr. Manju: Smoking and alcohol to be avoided. No drugs to be taken without prescription, especially skin-related products. General health check for both partners is a good idea.

Author Radhika: What should one know before trying to conceive?

Dr. Manju: You should know and understand that the fertile period and probability of conception in each month is only 15%. Couples can go for preconception counselling.

Author Radhika: If a woman had a miscarriage once, can she try again for pregnancy?

Dr. Manju: Of course; after 3-6 months.

Author Radhika: Is there anything off-limits in the sex department, that is, can couples enjoy their intimate time during the pregnancy?

Dr. Manju: After three months of conceiving but only if the doctor allows as it depends on various factors.

Author Radhika: How does my weight affect my pregnancy?

Dr. Manju: Being overweight makes one prone to diabetes and high blood pressure on pregnancy so it is always better to start your pregnancy journey with an optimum body weight.

Author Radhika: What can we do to avoid miscarriage?

Dr. Manju: Regular check-ups at right time, right medicines as prescribed by the doctor, and tests as prescribed are a must. However, despite taking all precautions, sometimes, some are unavoidable.

Author Radhika: Any advice/suggestion for first-time expectant couples?

Dr. Manju: Destress yourself and give time to yourself. Do not worry about everything that people advice you about. Just follow instructions of the doctor regarding check-ups and supplements, etc. and carry on life as normal. Pregnancy is one of the best periods of life for both parents. Enjoy it.

Key Takeaways:

- Missed periods of more than 40 days must be tested for pregnancy using Urine Pregnancy Test.

- If the pregnancy test is found to be positive, it has to be confirmed by a gynaecologist
- While trying to conceive, the following are important: healthy eating habits, weight reduction, physical exercise, positive mindset and attitude
- Rule out PCOS if you haven't been able to concieve
- Keep a Journal of your pregnancy

The Three Trimesters: Your Health, Exercise And Diet Plans

"Carrying A Baby Is The Most Rewarding Experience A Woman Can Enjoy." – Jayne Mansfield

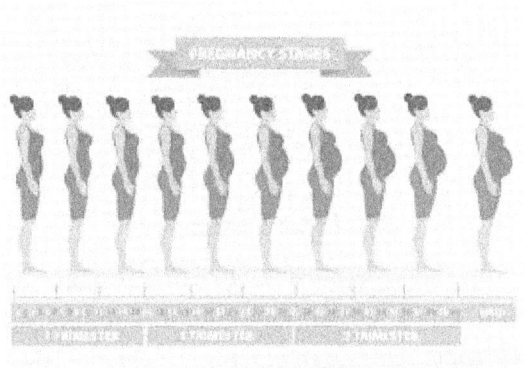

It's an amazing feeling when you first hear the heartbeat of a new life inside you during your first ultrasound check-up. You won't feel any movement as yet but yes! A new life is growing inside you. And this will be very evident to you in so many ways. Your skin will glow (get ready for compliments), you may feel tired so sleep as much as you like, you will be extra-sensitive to certain smells. A favorite perfume may make you want to throw up but hey, it's all good. You're two now. Your doctor will give you a due date, the date of the arrival of your baby into this world, based on the date of your last period. This will be confirmed by the ultrasound report but remember, each baby is different so treat this as an approximate date. The actual date may be earlier or a bit later than the given date.

The pregnancy phase is divided into three trimesters:

1. First Trimester (1 week - 12 weeks)
2. Second Trimester (13 weeks - 27 weeks)
3. Third Trimester (28 weeks - 40 weeks)

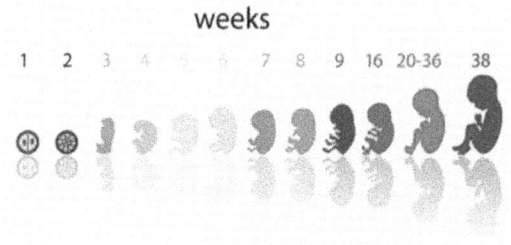

The First Trimester

Your love is not outside; it is deep within you. You can never lose it, and it cannot leave you. It is not dependent on some other body, some external form. - Eckhart Tolle

Now, let's discuss what all can you expect in the first trimester, how to keep yourself fit physically and mentally, and what would be a healthy diet for you. Most importantly, how can you take care of yourself?

In the first trimester, you can expect nausea, tiredness, and the loss of appetite, etc. However, some moms-to-be have morning sickness, some sail through without any hint of it; some moms feel like sleeping all the time, others don't. So, listen to your body and consult your doctor for any extreme tendencies.

In my case, I remember, I used to feel sleepy a lot even after sleeping for 10 hours at night. My body used to feel tired. My gynae suggested I should add more protein in my food diet. It's better to eat something like a banana, dry fruits (almond, walnut) once you wake up.

Your Baby's Growth In The First-Trimester

The foetus or your baby grows every day. By the end of week 4, it is very, very tiny, just the size of a poppy seed and by the end of week 12, it will be the size of a plum. After about 12 days of pregnancy, your baby grows within the amniotic sac which is filled with the amniotic fluid. This protects the embryo. Nuchal translucency scan is done at the end of 12 weeks to assess the neural tube defects in the child.

Doctors can make out the sex of the baby as early as 14 weeks but in India it is a punishable offence to ask about the gender or for the doctor or nurse to tell you. So please do not ask. Wait for the surprise. In other countries like USA, etc. it's revealed before the baby is born. But when the gender is unknown, the excitement is more, and you keep planning and thinking about both. Conversations with your partner may be about tentative names and so on. These are exciting days, happy days, and enjoy every minute of it. For example, you may say if it is a boy, then his name will be such and such; or your husband or partner may say, if it's a girl, her room should be in this colour, and so on. Gone are those days when blue used to be for boys and pink for girls. Parents now paint nurseries in yellow, green, white, etc and the clothes are also in various subtle colors that are gender neutral.

Your Body In The First Trimester

You can expect bloating, mild bleeding, cramping and mood swings in the first three months. At this time, you might feel a lack of concentration, forgetfulness, mood swings, etc. Keep yourself productive and engaged in the work that you enjoy the most. Listen to music, read books, relax.

Let's look at some physical changes that take place in your body during this trimester.

Vaginal discharge: You may have a thick whitish discharge from your vagina. This is normal but if it is excessive or if it bothers you in any way like itching, etc., get in touch with the doctor. You may get mild spotting or a light bleed. Even though it may not be anything to worry about, consult your doctor immediately. He or she may advice bedrest if needed and may prescribe some medication.

Fatigue: Your body is already doing so much work while offering the blood supply to the developing baby. You might feel tired a lot. You shouldn't stress out during this time and ensure that you're getting enough sleep.

Morning Sickness: This is a common symptom in new expecting mothers. You might feel nausea, vomiting, etc. Some moms-to-be feel sick throughout the day, not just in the morning, and others don't feel sick at all. As suggested earlier, eat dry fruits just after you wake up and then leave the bed to start your day. The best thing is that these symptoms disappear once you enter into the second trimester.

Frequent urination: This is caused by the uterus putting pressure on the bladder. This is normal. There are times when you will have to take many loo breaks during a car trip. Just enjoy the ride and store these memories to smile at later.

There are a few other common symptoms that you can feel in this pregnancy phase like constipation, heartburn, breast changes, gum infection, and varicose veins. It varies from person to person. Some might feel changes a little earlier and some may not feel it much. Breasts will become a bit bigger and nipples may ache but this is because of hormonal changes and won't bother you so much. If anything bothers you, I can't repeat it enough, call your doctor to understand better.

Healthy Diet Suggestions For First Trimester

- Coconut water
- Eat dry fruits (Almonds and Walnuts) after rising.
- Avoid Junk Food
- Avoid Spicy Food
- Eat more protein: Protein should be taken for the growth and the protection of the foetus. In vegetarian diet plan, proteins are found in dal, mushrooms, paneer, peas, etc.
- Have a nutrient-rich diet. You can take in folic acid from natural foods like beetroot, seasonal vegetables and cooked lentils - moong dal. So, don't forget to

take dahi, chaas and again the soaked, sprouted and well-cooked lentils.

A Sample Menu for a Day in the First Trimester

Timing	Meals
Wake up	Dried figs/fresh fruit
Breakfast (within 90 minutes)	Poha/Jowar flakes/daliya
Mid-Morning	Coconut water
Lunch	Roti + sabzi + buttermilk or Dal, rice and sabzi
Hi-tea	Tea with foxnuts, ladoo or egg toast
Dinner	Khichadi/ragi dosa/lentils +homemade pickle
Bedtime	A cup of milk with haldi

Reference has been taken from the book "Pregnancy notes" by Rujuta Diwekar. Follow her book to know about healthy ingredients recipes.

Exercising In The First Trimester

It is best to avoid vigorous exercise in the first trimester but listen to the doctor. If he or she says it is ok, go for it. The best ways to keep yourself fit in this trimester is by *walking, swimming and yoga*. Swimming is a fantastic way of relaxing your body and soothing your anxiety in this trimester. However, do consult your doctor. Skipping, hopping, sit-ups, etc. should be avoided. You can also put on music and swing along to it. As long as your dancing does not involve sudden movements, it will be good for you and relax you.

Also, exercise only if you want to. If your body says no, listen to it. Pamper yourself like a queen because that's what you are!

Expert Interview

Dental check-up is very important in pregnancy especially in the first trimester. Interview with Dr. Charu, a senior dental surgeon at World of Dentistry, Sector 46 Gurgaon, and a mother of a 4 years old girl.

Author Radhika: How can a dentist help a mother-to-be?

Dr. Charu: We help and guide all expectant mums to maintain their oral health and even for their dental needs. It is advised to get your assessment of oral health and map out a dental plan for the better treatment. You can contact me via phone (+91-8373962491) with the reference of "Radhika Jindal".

Dental health plays an important role during the pregnancy. Make sure you brush your teeth regularly and keep them clean. Floss at least weekly is not daily. Have a dental check-up early on in your pregnancy to avoid any complications as painkillers, etc. should be avoided as far as possible during pregnancy, and to do this, you need to avoid toothache as far as possible.

Author Radhika: Is dental checkup important for the expecting mothers? If yes, why?

Dr. Charu: Due to the abrupt hormonal changes, pregnant women are susceptible to the wide range of oral health conditions that could be harmful to their oral health and future of their baby so dental checkup is mandatory

Author Radhika: What's the one thing that an expecting mother shouldn't avoid to maintain oral hygiene?

Dr. Charu: Brushing twice a day

Author Radhika: What are the common dental problems faced during the pregnancy?

Dr. Charu: Bleeding gums, tooth decay, erosion of enamel, dry mouth and bad breath due to decrease in saliva.

Author Radhika: What problems can an expectant mom face due to bad oral health?

Dr. Charu: Bad oral health in pregnancy doesn't only cause problems such as tooth decay and tooth loss but also lead to premature birth, low birth weight infants, and pre-eclampsia

Author Radhika: What are periodontal diseases? How can we deal with it?

Dr. Charu: Periodontal disease is a gum infection that damages the gums and can affect the gum bone and even soft tissue of mouth. This can be dealt with by regular scaling and polishing during dental checkups.

Author Radhika: What is the importance of nutrition on dental health during pregnancy?

Dr. Charu: Adequate intake of nutrients contributes to positive effects on the mother and the foetus health. It is necessary to take 1200 to 1500 MG daily calcium for herself and babies bones to be healthy. This can be done by incorporating green leafy vegetables, dairy products, and milk in your diet. Babies tooth development starts in 5th and 6th week of pregnancy. Avoid sugar in access to prevent any tooth decay.

Author Radhika: What type of balanced diet is recommended to maintain oral/dental health?

Dr. Charu: Fruits, vegetables, cereal, milk and dairy products, fish, and eggs that provide vitamin A, C, and D, calcium, and phosphorus must be taken in a balanced diet. Sugar, including caramel and toffees, should be avoided and as much as possible shift to jaggery. Vitamin A and D helps in enamel formation

Author Radhika: How is alcohol consumption bad for dental health during pregnancy?

Dr. Charu: Consumption of alcohol in pregnancy leads to teratogenic effects and cause fetal alcohol syndrome that leads to dental anomalies, structural deterioration of enamel, and delayed eruption of teeth.

A few important things to remember:

- Always take supplements like iron, calcium, folic acid and protein on time. These supplements will continue even after the delivery depending on what your doctor suggests.
- A supplement is never a replacement to eating right, exercising and sleeping on time. You must follow a positive attitude towards life.
- Be in touch with your gynae all the time. Never hesitate to ask anything and sharing your feelings.
- You will be advised to drink a minimum three litres of liquid in a day including milk, juices, and shakes etc.
- Try to be active physically and mentally.
- The most important, is to "take proper rest". Never be hard on yourself. If you feel like you want to take a quick short nap, please do that.
- Don't stress out yourself.
- Don't drink tea/coffee for the first two hours after rising.

Now! Congratulations on completing your first trimester.

The Second Trimester

"A baby will make love stronger, days shorter, nights longer, bankroll smaller, home happier, clothes shabbier, the past forgotten, and the future worth living for." – Anonymous

Now, you might get some relief from pregnancy symptoms like morning sickness and fatigue etc. Along with the baby gaining weight, you are also putting on. But, don't worry! Be happy. Just try to eat healthy. Feel proud that you're gaining weight because of some good reasons. You can later shed the weight. Now, it's the time to eat and be healthier. You can check your babycentre app, or any other app you have registered in, to know more about the growth of your foetus. By 18 weeks, the foetus is the size of bell pepper, height is five and a half inches, weight is .20kg.

There're a few exercises that are especially designed for the expecting mothers. Consult your doctor and do them under proper guidance and observation. A few I would like to mention include Kegel exercise, Lamaze, Prenatal Yoga, and different types of breathing techniques. Breathing plays a crucial role during labour that needs to be practiced properly. We'll be discussing it in the later chapters.

You can find out more about these exercises or you can join a mothers' club either near you or online and stay in touch with other mothers. Mostly, it is seen, expecting mothers feel more energetic and have a jovial mood during this trimester.

In between 18 to 20th weeks, you'll have your third ultrasound, known as "Anatomy scan". The ultrasound is performed to check the development of fetal structures such as spine, limbs, and brain etc. The size of the placenta is also checked. By this time, the genital organs of the baby are developed properly. Your baby starts listening to various sounds such as your breathing, heartbeat, and speaking tone. This is the best time to apply *garbh sanskar*. We'll be discussing more about this in detail in the next chapter. In your ultrasound visit, you can ask your radiologist or doctor to show you the baby's hands, legs, face on the screen. It's such an awesome feeling that it can't be expressed in words. You must feel proud and extremely happy that your baby is growing well inside you.

In this trimester, you can feel the foetus's hiccups too. The baby makes movements like kicking, bending the limbs and the joints, crossing the legs, etc. They will also do kicking, twisting, tumbling and rolling around and holding the umbilical cord sometimes. All these you will be able to feel from the fifth month onward. By the sixth month, you can expect kicks from the baby. That simply means the baby is playing and moving inside. It is such a miracle when you or your partner can feel the kick of your baby inside you. Kicks indicate that the baby is responding to you.

Babies are mostly active during the night when it's the best time and you're also calm. Try to make time and talk to your baby. Just feel their kicks and enjoy the moment with your partner. Let him also feel the vibes.

Note: Sometimes, if you don't feel the kicks, don't be over-stressed. Your unborn baby might be sleeping. But you do need to monitor it sometime. If you do not feel movement for a while, you can drink cold water, some sweet tea, rub your belly a little or lie down on your left side to feel the kicks of the baby. Please have patience and be calm while you're just focusing on the kicks. There shouldn't be any kind of disturbance. If you feel movement is low, please immediately contact your doctor just to be on the safe side.

By the 22nd week, your baby is the size of a papaya. By the 25th week, the foetus growth rate is high. At this time, the length is 13 and half inches and weight is around 0.680389 kg (1 ½ pounds). Now, you can expect your weight and breast size to increase a little. Invest in some good maternity clothes. Always choose loose and comfortable clothes. You can check out online shopping websites like Myntra, Amazon, etc. Many brands such as H&M, Mom & Me, Mothercare, have plenty of choice for maternity wear.

Your Body In The Second Trimester

1. Discharge: Vaginal infection is common during pregnancy. Make sure that you're following basic hygiene and keeping the vaginal area clean. Vaginal infection or itching is common during and after the pregnancy.

2. Colostrum's leak: As your breasts are growing, you may feel tender breasts. Your breast might leak a creamy yellowish color syrup or "colostrum" as the body prepares itself for the breastfeeding. You can use breast pads inside your bra if you feel it is leaking.

3. Pain: Pregnancy symptoms like aches and pains may arise from baby's movements. Mild pain is common. You can consult your gynae if the pain is unbearable or if you feel uncomfortable.

4. Braxton hick's contractions: Second trimester is too early for contractions but you can feel it sometimes. These are called Braxton-Hicks contractions and are false contractions. However, you need to be in touch with your doctor for the right suggestion.

5. Skin changes: In a few pregnancy cases, expecting mothers may feel their skin is getting darker. I remember in my case, it wasn't much but yes, my friends experienced this. So, nothing to worry about, it'll disappear after the delivery and with time.

6. Swelling and fluid retention: This is again common during the 2nd trimester of pregnancy. Many mothers feel they have swelling on their face and legs etc. But again, it varies from person to person. Women who are short in height have more chances of getting swelling. Make sure that you're taking proper rest after every one hour. You can dip your feet in the lukewarm water and keep sitting for 10 minutes. It'll make you feel relaxed. Keep your feet up straight while sitting as this will help. You should try walking after every half an hour for 10-15 minutes at least.

7. Constipation: Yes! This is another common issue in pregnancy which mostly all moms experience. Here is how you can deal with it? Drink a glass of warm water before every meal. You can also have half tsp of gulkand after every meal.

8. Backache: As we all know, by now, your foetus is growing day by day. As you are supporting it inside you, you may have back pain. Here are a few suggestions you can try that will reduce the back pain.

- Learn to stand correctly and balance your weight on your two feet.

- A few Yoga poses like cat/cow pose, corpse pose and the mountain pose, etc., will help you to maintain your posture.
- Use a footstool for your legs while working on the desk.
- Drink enough water, but drink less tea/coffee/colas.
- Don't sit/stand at a place for a long period of time.

Note: You must check out the book "Iyengar Yoga by for Motherhood".

Healthy Diet Suggestions For Second Trimester

Ladoos can be made with dry fruits and seeds. They will give you a lot of energy as well as protein and calcium during pregnancy. Here is one recipe that you can use:

Ingredients:

- Whole Wheat Flour
- Ghee
- Jaggery powder
- Pumpkin seeds
- Muskmelon Seeds
- Chia seeds
- Almond Powder (Roast Mamra Almonds and then grind it), it's rich in omega fatty acids.
- Lotus seeds powder (roast it and then grind), it has more calcium.

Note: Don't eat gond (edible gum) during the entire pregnancy. You can add coconut powder while making the ladoos if you like this flavour.

How to make it:

Add Ghee and roast wheat flour until it becomes brown in color.

Add almond powder, lotus seeds powder and all the seeds.

Mix it well and add jaggery powder in the end.

Let it be cool for sometimes and then form into the shape of ladoos.

You can eat it anytime of the day. They're good. The receipe is shared by my mother-in-law.

Travel by Air Personal Experience: I remember my second trimester when I had to travel via flight to Ahmedabad to attend a function. I was five months pregnant and my reports were normal. Generally doctors don't allow you to travel via flights during the entire pregnancy but it depends on your medical history too and how much you're able to manage with it. My gynaecologist allowed me to travel and suggested a few things to take care. I would like to share this with you all.

1. Take snacks with you like roasted lotus seeds, baked cookies, dry fruits like raisins, walnut , roasted almonds and cashew nuts.

2. Carry your water bottle with you.

3. Wear comfortable sports shoes. Walk slowly and try to maintain the balance.

4. Don't rush. Just keep everything ready before you leave.

5. Put on some music that makes you feel relax.

Driving License personal experience: I remember the time when I went for driving license before I was expecting. I cleared the first test and got the Trial Driving license that is valid for six months. I conceived after a month of clearing the tests but I had only five months to clear the final round. I knew basic driving but my husband put in the best efforts and helped me to learn so many things in a less time. It was my fifth month of pregnancy, when I went to give the final round but I got nervous and couldn't clear the round. We both knew, once we have the baby, it'll be difficult to apply for the same. So, we filled up the form again and did all the formalities related to the documents. Again I started everything afresh and with a mindset that this time I have to put in my best efforts. I practiced a lot for 1-2 hours daily. I practiced my control on the break and reverse, and remembering to horn and use the right indicator, and of course the seat belt that is noticed at first glance.

I am thankful to god, my husband is a calm and a hardworking person whereas I become little impatient sometimes. He made me feel comfortable at every step during the driving practicing session so, that it wouldn't affect the baby. I would have taken the homemade snacks along with me during the practice and kept myself hydrated. This way, I was able to cope up with the pressure of clearing the driving tests.

A few important things to remember:

- Testing for diabetes in pregnancy
- Screening for Down syndrome, if not done in the first-trimester
- Avoid wearing high heels from now onwards.
- Don't stand for long period of time. Try to use the stool while sitting.
- You can expect a few stretch marks now; start applying a good moisturizing cream.
- Don't worry about the weight gain, just try to maintain a healthy balanced diet.
- Use Nutmeg (Jaiphal)
- Include ghee a little more as it helps to support the insulin function
- Use millets like Foxtail millet, Finger millet, etc. They're gluten-free.

Now, congratulations on completing your first two trimesters. Hurray!

The Third Trimester

"Everything grows rounder and wider and weirder, and I sit here in the middle of it all and wonder who in the world you will turn out to be." – Carrie Fisher

In the 7th month, your ultrasound will be performed after 30 weeks to check the baby's growth. The placenta will be checked to see it's not blocking the cervix. There's a risk if the baby gets delivered this month because the lungs are not yet mature. The babies who gets delivered in this month are called "premature" babies. They're kept in NICU to treat them properly.

Everything takes its own time to get into the shape like, that same way, the foetus is taking his time to grow.

In this month, a lot of things will start happening. It might be a little difficult for you to take long breaths and it's better to take short deep breaths. You can expect the belly bump to show more now. Show off your baby tummy and feel proud you're going to be a mother soon. Many people have a baby moon in this month nowadays when they go for a holiday to relax themselves before the baby comes. Baby is more active during this time. Please make sure that you feel your baby's kicks after breakfast, lunch and dinner, etc. If you don't feel anything, you can have a talk with your gynae. You can ask your baby whether he liked the food, yes! Baby is listening to you. The foetus also tastes the food through the placenta.

By the eight month, the foetus brain is develops fast. You shouldn't travel much this month onwards to be on safer side. In this month, the foetus weight should be approximately 2.2 kgs, and is the size of a small watermelon. However, all babies are different and being healthy with good movement is all that matters. The body parts are developing this month. It is advisable for the mother keeps herself calm and productive. You can try out reading good pregnancy books, or any genre you like. You can listen to pleasant music and do activities you enjoy the most, like Mandala coloring, etc. Go for walks because this will help your muscles during labour and also keep circulation good.

Your Body In The Third Trimester

Heartburn: Sleep on your left side. This will help prevent heart burn. Here are a few tips:

- Avoid spicy food
- Avoid junk food/oily/gassy food
- Drink more water
- Eat less spicy vegetable
- Walk
- Drink warm water before food

Tingling and numbness: You may feel tingling sensation on your feet or hands. Don't worry this is because the swelling in your body may be pressing on nerves. This will stop after the delivery. This may also cause itching.

Stretching of skin: Moisturize your tummy and gently rub oil on it so that it remains smooth. Stretch marks are a proud sign of being a mother but doing this will minimize the marks.

Swelling: As we have already discussed, there will be swelling in many mothers. This is usually nothing to worry about but in case it becomes very uncomfortable and you are seeing blurred vision, lease get in touch with the doctor.

Healthy Diet For Third Trimester

- Coconut water
- Eat dry fruits (Almonds and Walnuts)
- Adding nutmeg and ghee to food will be good.
- Spinach, sweet potato, carrots, fish are all rich in Vitamin A, which will help the babies eyes, bones, and skin.
- Tomatoes, oranges, broccoli will provide Vitamin C
- Bananas, potatoes, fish, etc., will give you Vitamin B6 for brain development of your baby
- Eggs and dairy products will help provide Vitamin B12 for your baby's nervous system.
- If you are vegetarian, you will need a Vitamin B12 supplement.
- Cheese, milk products and sunlight will help with Vitamin D for strong bones.
- Calcium too will come from milk products and broccoli.
- Have iron rich food like spinach and nuts.

Exercising In The Third Trimester

The last month is more crucial and the last month of pregnancy. You're counting every day now before your delivery day. The reverse counting has started. The foetus's weight should be around or more than 2.7 kgs. Here are a few exercises you can do now:

Pelvic floor exercise / Kegeal exercise : This exercise is performed to strengthen the pelvic muscles. Once you know which muscles  (consult your doctor for this to understand better) to target, you can do it any time of the day. You can practice the basic by contracting these muscles for 5 to 10 seconds and then release it. Then, repeating the same things again for 5-10minutes at one time.

Butterfly pose (2mins): This is also known as Badhakonasana in Sanskrit and the bound Angel pose in English. This is another powerful exercise to be performed during pregnancy to strengthen the lower back, hips and inner thigh. It helps in increasing the flexibility. It is much helpful in stretching and opening up the hips, and  the pelvic muscles. This exercise works wonder to prepare oneself for the normal delivery.

Squatting (half): This is helpful in improving blood circulation and improves hip mobility. This exercise is done in the last phase of

pregnancy only. This is the most highly recommended exercise to perform with your partner in the last month. This helps in preparing for the labour. Kindly consult your prenatal expert for all the exercise to do it properly.

Perineal massage: The delicate area between the anus and the vagina is called the perineum. This area is stretched during the labour time, but regular massage can help in preventing a tear in the perineum. There's nothing to shy while doing this as you're putting in your best efforts to prepare for the delivery day.

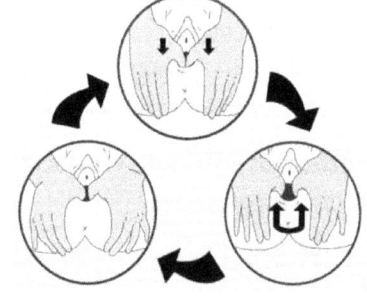

There are many other exercises to be performed to prepare yourself best for labour. You can check out Nutan Pandit's books and videos on YouTube to educate yourself.

In this last month, you'll find it a little difficult to take side turns, lots of heartburn and mood swings.

Expert Interview

Interview with Dr. Shilpi Srivastav, consultant with Sitaram Bhartiya Iinstitute of science and research Delhi and Motherhood Hospital, Noida. (Women's health physiotherapist, lactation counsellor, Lamaze certified childbirth educator, birth doula, prenatal yoga instructor and a mom of 6 years old girl, with an extensive experience of 10 years)

Author Radhika: How can you help a new mother?

Dr. Shilpi: Pregnancy is a beautiful journey. It comes with lots of queries and anxiety. I can help expecting couples and new parents by keeping them emotionally and physically fit. And by providing them informed choices and enhancing the pregnancy and birthing experience. You can reach me via email at momleycare@gmail.com. Give the reference "Radhika Jindal".

Author Radhika: Please throw some light on the terms like Prenatal, Antenatal and Perinatal?
Dr. Shilpi: prenatal or antenatal is the pregnancy period. Perinatal refers to period around birth.

Author Radhika: What's the right time to join these specific programmes?

Dr. Shilpi: Fitness or yoga can be joined in first trimester if you have low risk pregnancy. Your obgyn consult is required. Safe time to join yoga and fitness is post 12 weeks or once your level one ultrasound is done.

Author Radhika: How will joining prenatal classes be helpful to the expectant mothers?

Dr. Shilpi: Fitness is important for all. During pregnancy fitness plays an important role in keeping mom and baby healthy.

Author Radhika: How can a new mother take care of herself after the delivery?

Dr. Shilpi: Preparation is the key. Attending Lamaze classes prepares a couple for delivery and postpartum, that is postdelivery.

Author Radhika: please throw some light on Lamaze and Kegel exercise? When should one start practicing this?
Dr. Shilpi: Lamaze classes are kind of childbirth

preparation classes where both the partners are prepared for the labour pain. Husband also plays an important role. He learns how he can support the lady, how she can cope up with the process,s and what are the expectations from the labour. Lamaze classes are taken ideally in seven months. It makes you prepare for the delivery and initial first few months and how you are going to take care of the newborn. Breastfeeding guidance is also given along with this. Kegel is important exercise for females. It is guided by the physiotherapist. This is done to strengthen the pelvic floor muscles. It can only be done by the specialist.

Author Radhika: When should one start doing exercise to stay physically fit?

Dr. Shilpi: Exercise during pregnancy should be started soon if you're physically fit and have low risk pregnancy. Else, it is recommended to start from 2nd trimester of pregnancy.

Author Radhika: Any suggestions on the types of exercise for preparing for the normal delivery especially in the last trimester of the pregnancy?

Dr. Shipli: Staying fit throughout the pregnancy, being physically and mentally fit for the pregnancy, choosing the right doctor is important. You can start a few exercises in the third trimester like cat and camel pose, duck pose, squats, lunges, and walk for at least one hour in a day.

Things to Avoid:

Unpurified water

Travelling

Driving

Dancing

Pushups

Raw vegetables as far as possible

Alcohol and smoking absolutely no.

Raw sprouts

Do not lift anything heavy now

Now is the time to keep a bag ready for the hospital. Pack a few things for your baby too. Be cool and calm. Don't stop walking but like in the first trimester, please do rest when you feel tired. After the baby is here, you won't get much rest! Just hang on there…just a little more time for your baby to be with you!

BOOKS RECOMMENDATIONS:
1. Pregnancy Notes by Rujuta Diwekar (for meal plans)
2. Nutun Pandit's books

Key Takeaways:

Important Scans during pregnancy

- 1st scan at 6 weeks for confirmation of pregnancy
- 2nd Scan at 11-13 weeks to rule out neural tube defects
- 3rd Scan at 18-21weeks anomaly scan to rule out fetal anomalies
- 4th Scan at around 28 weeks - growth scan

- 5th Scan nearing delivery date to check for fetal engagement in pelvis, amniotic fluid levels, position of the baby.

These five scans are mandatory to check the baby's growth.

Red Signs during pregnancy

1st trimester
- severe vomiting
- bleeding per vagina
- lower pain abdominal

2nd trimester :
- unable to feel movements even after 22 weeks of pregnancy
- bleeding per vagina
- giddiness
- severe headache
- lower abdominal pain
- palpitations

3rd trimester
- not able to feel kicks for more than a hour or two.
- leaking per vagina
- bleeding per vagina
- firm contractions at regular intervals

Diet

- avoid spicy and oily food
- drink around 3 litres of water
- diet rich in calories , proteins and dietary fibres is needed

(additional 1000 calories is required apart of routine intake)

Emotional health

Your emotional health is equally important to that of your physical health. Keep yourself happy, positive and relaxed throughout your pregnancy. Prepare yourself to the additional set of responsibilities once the baby is born.

3
Garbh Sanskar

"Making the decision to have a child is momentous. It is to decide forever to have your heart go walking around outside your body." – Elizabeth Stone

One thing that I did not know much about during my pregnancy days was Garbh Sanskar. I regret not being aware of it during that time but I practiced it in my own way by staying positive. I performed chanting and listened to relaxing music to send positive vibrations to the foetus in the womb. Similar to me, mothers in all cultures of the world are told to think happy thoughts, talk and read to their baby inside them. There are different traditions in different communities which encourage this. In India, Garbh Sanskar dates back to the Vedic Age. However, we now know that there is also a scientific basis for doing this. There are workshops and sessions on Garbh Sanskar and as a mother-to-be, this is the best way you can give your child a happy and healthy start to his or her life.

The term "Sanskar" means values, karmas, belief, thoughts. It varies from person to person depending on their culture, experience, and behavior. It refers to the upbringing of a person and his or her psychological imprints or mental recollections. A person's sanskar or upbringing that is shown outside comes from within the subconscious mind, and most of these behaviors are already formed before birth. The word "garbh" refers to "foetus in the womb". Thus Garbh Sanskar means "education of the mind of the foetus".

There is scientific evidence that proves that Garbh Sanskar determines the health of a child. The mother's emotional state of mind influences it while she carries the baby. "During pregnancy, there is constant communication between maternal and fetal cells," says senior author Ramkumar Menon, UTMB associate professor in the department of obstetrics and gynecology. Garbh Sanskar plays a crucial role in building up the mental and physical wellbeing of an unborn child. This is only possible when the mother follows her daily practice in various forms.

If a mother is happy and has positive thoughts during her pregnancy, then it'll have a positive impact on the foetus. When a mother feels happy and cheerful, she releases oxytocin hormones and the baby thereby understands the feelings of a mother. By the time, the baby is three months inside the womb; he or she starts recognizing taste, sound, and smell. Many times, you will see that the baby is able to recognise your voice. For example, when there is too much movement, talking soothingly in your voice will help calm the baby down.

Pregnancy is the most beautiful phase in a woman's life. Following the process of Garbh Sanskar, a mother-to-be will be able to derive the maximum benefit to both herself and her child.

Benefits of Garbh Sanskar

- It develops the bond of mother-child
- It promotes good physical well-being
- It helps in the development of the baby's brain - Adverse nutrition or mental state of mother during pregnancy can permanently affect the baby's brain development.
- It keeps the baby calm and happy.

How A Mother Can Practice Garbh Sanskar

Garbh Sanskar involves good nutrition for the baby, positive attitude and healthy behavior through yoga or other physical activity, as well as good education and good thoughts through talking to your baby, reading aloud or listening to music or talks. As we have already discussed other healthy habits of nutrition and exercise, let us look at a few ways in which a mother-to-be can practice Garbh Sanskar through communication with the foetus.

Yoga and music therapy: To a foetus, a mother's voice is clearer than any other voice. Through Garbh Samvad (specific guided meditation to be performed during the pregnancy), you can talk to the baby in the womb.

Om chanting: The child feels the calming energy and has a positive vibration when a mother chants "OM". It's better to perform it every morning just after you wake up or in the night before sleeping.

Positive self-talk: You need to understand that your child is listening to you every single second. They can't express, but they can feel. Talk to yourself in a soothing voice, address your child, feel one with him or her.

Journaling: You can sit with your husband or partner and write all the wonderful qualities that you want in your baby. Take a printout and post it on the wall or where it will be the most visible. Be specific while mentioning. For example, you may write: intelligent, dancer, spiritual, and positive attitude, etc.

Garbh Sanskar is for all those women who are going to be a mother. She can perform this anytime and anywhere. But to get the best results, they should practice it daily at a specific time.

The Importance Of Visualization

We all are aware how much the Covid-19 has affected us, especially the expecting mothers in the last one year and it's not over yet. It has affected people both physically and mentally. Apart from Covid, there are disturbing news and opinions available everyday on TV or on social media. In such situations, it is difficult to keep your mind calm and relaxed, especially when you are expecting your baby.

However, despite everything, we all have something to be grateful for, and the most important reason is that you are about to be a mother of a precious new being on earth. What could be more auspicious than that? So, let's take out some time today to thank the power of the universe and be grateful to God for showering his blessings upon us.

First, be calm and sit in a quiet environment.

Take a deep breath and make yourself calm and relaxed.

Forget everything for a while and just bring all your focus on the things which you are grateful for. Have you heard about Affirmations? Affirmations are a great way to think positively in any situation. It can help the mother turn negative feelings related to pregnancy into positive ones. You can practice it anytime of the day but with full positive intention and turning them into actual beliefs over me. As an expecting mother, you can try out some positive affirmations as follows:

I accept the positive changes in my body.

I am healthy

My pregnant body is beautiful.

My baby is perfectly healthy.

Thank you God for the foetus heartbeat.

Thank you universe for the positive vibes.

Thank you universe for all the healing powers.

I am grateful to God for the positive changes.

I am grateful to my family for their unconditional love.

I am grateful to my doctor for his/her guidance.

I am grateful to my parents for always being with me.

I am grateful for everyone around me.

I am grateful to my husband for always supporting me.

(Affirmations by Deepak Devaraj, author of *The Power of Thoughts and Visualizations* and *Unlimited Energy* and the father of 5 years old girl)

You can keep on adding to the list and making your own affirmations. Just do it with the power of intention. Feel it. To get the best out of it, you can take a photograph of your affirmations and use it on your phone wallpaper or keep it on your desk or in the kitchen, wherever it's more visible.

This will help you in rewiring your brain and also would help in reducing stress and anxiety.

Talking To Your Baby Inside You

Since you are now carrying one more life in you, it's important for expecting mothers to feel happy both inside and outside. If a mother is happy and in a calm state, she will have a positive impact on the foetus. Don't forget, the unborn child can feel all your emotions within you.

So, let's do a little visualization by being in a peaceful state.

Allow yourself to take a break at least for a minimum of 5 minutes...

Just be comfortable. Close your eyes.

Are you ready to talk to your unborn child? So let's begin.

Mother: How are you, my baby?

The Foetus: I'm rocking, mumma. Hope you're cool too.

Mother: So, how are you feeling now?

The Foetus: Feeling fabulous to see you relaxed mumma.

Mother: Do you like all the food served by me to you?

The Foetus: Yes mumma! except the spicy food.

Mother: What makes you happy?

The Foetus: When you're singing, painting, reading, writing, laughing, cooking and dancing, etc. and doing what keeps you happy, it makes me happy too.

So, what do you understand from the above conversation between the mother and the unborn baby?

This is something that we all do. We talk with our unborn child, sometimes aloud and some moms do it in their minds. Yes, I did it too. It may seem funny or embarrassing to share this with others but in fact, this is what builds the bond. There is scientific proof now that the unborn baby can hear you, and can feel your emotions well.

A Visualization And Communication Exercise

Now, let us go deeper. Visualization has the power to turn your mindset into a positive one and can actually give us a desired situation and take us where we want to be.

Sit or lie down in a quiet place and close your eyes. Imagine that you are already holding your baby in your hands. You feel a sense of both excitement and nervousness. You thank God for blessing you with a cute baby. See in your mind that you are smiling and shedding tears of joy after seeing your little one. You are observing those tiny fingers, tiny toes and enjoying the cuteness of the baby. Being with the baby, you forget to keep track of the time. You say to yourself that all other work and commitments can wait for some time while I play with my cute little baby.

The baby has taken all the stress away from you and just started giggling with you. The baby is looking into your eyes and trying to interact with you. It feels so good when the baby makes sounds like coo-coo and tries to involve us.

What else can you observe from the baby's eyes? Just focus...

You hear a cute voice from your baby, *"Thanks mumma for bringing me into this world with full of love and health. I am excited to walk on the path of my life with you, papa, dada, dadi, nana, nani, and everyone.*

Mumma, please don't get irritated, it makes me feel sad. Now, I have come into yours and papa's life to make your world beautiful and full of laughter. We are going to have fun every minute. Hahaha! Be ready to experience the roller-coaster ride."

Just be in the moment for some time. Observe your baby more. Talk to the baby. Convey your messages. Give your blessings. Sometimes, during this exercise, tears may flow from your eyes, Let it flow and don't pay attention. Slowly, move your toes and fingers. Now, rub your hands gently and place them on your eyes.

You can open your eyes now.

Hope you're feeling refreshed and more energetic now.

NAADI SIDDHI

This is a form of breathing technique of yoga. Mothers-to-be can practice different pranayamas as they feel comfortable, This helps in circulation and will not just relax them but will also help in sleep. Some mantras that can be chanted or listened to while doing this, including the Hanuman Chalisa. You can also listen to stories of men and women that you admire. Classical music also can be used in the background.

Books Recommendations

1. Talking to the baby in the womb by Dr. S. Andal Bhaskar
2. Garbh Sanskar - You Reap What You Sow by Dr. Devangi Jogal & Nilesh Jogal

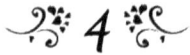

In-Laws And The Father-To-Be

"What good mothers and fathers instinctively feel like doing for their babies is usually best after all." — Benjamin Spock

The Role Of The Father

Gone are those days when the men used to work and the women used to stay at home and take care of the kids and the families. Now, both the partners share equal responsibility towards the child. But there are still a few families where the kids are taken care of solely by the mother only and the father's role is limited to earning for the family.

Planning a child is not one partner's decision, but of both. Just as a mother is overwhelmed by seeing those two lines in the pregnancy test, the father is equally excited to hear the news. It is as if the father too shares the pregnancy.

Some husbands are open-minded and well educated. They understand their women's concern and think about their health and future. A few men, however, cannot understand what their expectant wife is going through. Though she is going through a lot of pregnancy challenges like mood swings, gaining weight, feeling low, etc., some fathers-to-be move away from the wife during this time because they do not know how to handle the different changes. Also, some fathers-to-be get worried about the future with a child on the way and get busier with work.

> **Some Cute Ways To Announce The Pregnancy To Your Partner**
> - Arranging a candle light dinner
> - Write in a paper and keep it in the husband's lunch box
> - Write it on your tummy with the marker

The Role Of The Father

Respond appropriately to the news that your wife is pregnant. If you weren't planning on the arrival of a bundle of joy this early in the marriage, make sure you don't respond in a way that shows you're not excited about the news. For heaven's sake, don't ask her why did she not use birth control, for instance. You want your wife to feel confident and secure that you'll be there for her during these trying nine months and that you're willing to step up and be a great dad. Of course, in all probability, you will instantly jump for joy when you hear the news. Cheers! You are going to be a father!!!

The best way to learn about what the mother is going through or will go through is to read some books on pregnancy. The more you know about what she's going through, the better equipped you are to empathize and know how to help. There are hundreds of pregnancy books to choose from. *What to Expect When You're Expecting* is a classic and guides you through what your wife is experiencing during each step of her pregnancy. They have a section dedicated just to dads that has a lot of useful information. Dr Benjamin Spock's *Common Sense Book of Baby and Child Care* is another book that has been teaching generations of parents how to go through pregnancy and the early years of childcare.

I remember the time when I was five months pregnant. I used to go to the office with my husband. I would feel active for about half an hour and then suddenly my blood pressure would start getting low, and I would feel dull and exhausted. When I kept my head down to take a little rest, my husband couldn't understand why I was doing that. He expected me to be a little active in the office. Another incident was when I had a period of bad heartburn, especially at night, and I used to wake up. Heartburn mostly occurs because of the spicy food, fried food, etc. it can be prevented by drinking a lot of water and reducing the amount of spices. I used to sit for some time and eat the oranges, which I always kept on my side table. My husband would get annoyed because I kept moving around and ask me to sleep peacefully. There will be many circumstances like this which a father-to-be may not understand.

On the other hand, my husband was supportive in many things like coordination, managing household things together, staying organized, and spending quality time together. We discussed our own childhood and what all new changes we can expect after the delivery. We both knew that it would have some effects on our relationship too but we were prepared for it.

While the mother is going through a lot of challenges, the father equally goes through a lot of emotions and the fear of the responsibility of the child. The father can play a crucial role here like financial planning, medical check-ups, ultrasound screening, preparing the room for the new baby and maintaining a pleasant home environment

Here are a few tips on how a husband can be helpful/supportive to his wife during the pregnancy and support her in his own way.

- Accompany your wife for her antenatal check-ups: Be with her, hold her hand, look at the ultrasound videos together. This is a great time for bonding and making her feel safe.

- Monitor the wife's health and the diet: Remind her to drink water, keep track of the vitamins and any other medicine that the doctor may have prescribed, take her for walks.

- Share your thoughts: Do not close down. Share your day in the office or at work, ask her how she is feeling, listen to her. Communication should be both ways.

- Join prenatal classes: Join her for yoga or meditation classes, be there for birth preparation classes if you are taking them.

- Get involved in household chores: Pamper her, make her a cup of tea, cook for her, keep the house clean so that she doesn't have to go around picking up wet towels, etc.

- Go for shopping for baby items: This is something fun that both can do together. Choose clothes, toys, the baby's crib, etc.

- Book a holiday for her: Go on a trip that helps her relax. Just the two of you.

- Plan for the birth of the baby: Know the due date, the hospital contact details, the gynaecologist's number. Ask the doctor what will or may happen and be prepared.

- Provide emotional support: There are times when your wife may feel low, be there for her. There are times when she may want to talk, be there for her. Hold her, talk to her.

- Appreciate her new look of pregnancy: Admire her, tell her how good her skin looks, how proud you are of her.

- Encourage her: After seven to eight months of pregnancy, she may feel restless. Encourage her. Help her to overcome this feeling.

The In-Laws And The Roles They Play

Just as the first-time parents are excited, the in-laws on both sides are equally excited to become first-time grandparents. Undoubtedly, their time was different to what it is now. They were a little superstitious while today's generation is not. There are many rituals that take place during a pregnancy and the to-be grandparents, especially the to-be grandmothers, would be eager to carry them out. Do let them observe these traditions and rituals, and you will not just be giving them joy but also create memories for yourself.

There will come many times when the mother-in-law and daughter-in-law will disagree with each other. Here, the mother-in-law has to understand and remember how it was when she herself was pregnant, what she felt like, how tired she sometimes felt. As a modern grandmother-to-be, the best thing you can do is just to be a support in case you are asked for help. It is better not to interfere in the decisions of the young parents to be. Let your daughter-in-law or son-in-law go through the pregnancy in their own way. Give your advice when you think it is needed but do not get into arguments. The mom-to-be needs to stay relaxed and calm so that your grandchild gets the best start on life. Pamper her, go for a spa day together, cook her favourite meals, give her some me-time so that she can relax in her own way.

The father-in-laws can get involved in hospital visits, talking and sharing, etc. You can gift your daughter or daughter-in-law good books and music and discuss these with her, you can walk with her, be there for your son or son-in-law as a support.

How A Mother-In-Law Can Support The Expecting Daughter-In-Law?

- Taking care of her nutriotious diet: Don't force her to eat much but indeed she should eat healthy and balanced diet.

- Giving her "me-time": This plays a crucial role in de-stressing.

- Help in shopping: Helping her to find the right size of clothes that she may require in each trimester depending on the weather and the size.

- Allow to socialize: Allow her to make new friends and taking their suggestions on healthy pregnancy.
- Just be with her: She might not be able to express herself to you but she needs you at every step. You are her backbone. Whether you stay near or far to your kids, be with hereven if it via phone calls, enjoy a cup of tea together, etc.
- Don't pressurize her to attend family functions: She is already going through a lot of hormonal changes. So, don't force her to attend family functions if she is not comfortable. It's definitely her choice.
- Try to keep the environment happy: It's the best if you can keep the home environment happy and a relaxed place. Everyone should talk positive and feel happy around her.

A Token Of Love For My Husband, A Personal Experience

Jab tumhe paya,
toh ek sukoon sa mila,
Jab dia saath tumne,
Toh Khuda bhi mujhse khush hua

When I found you,
Then I found a kind of peace
When you stood beside me
Then God too was happy with me

If you're reading this book, then thanks to my husband from the bottom of my heart who supported me tremendously to write the book. He is always at my back and pushes me to move forward. I am thankful to him for always listening to me patiently and guiding me accordingly. We are the partners in crime. We both were excited as it was our first pregnancy and there were so many new things to explore for being a first time parent. I hope our bond remains the same forever and have the mutual understanding to plan for the second pregnancy too.

Key takeaways:
1. Speak your heart out with your loving husband.
2. Do what makes you feel comfortable.
3. Take elders advice; they are the experienced ones.
4. Pregnancy is meant to enjoy, not to stress yourself.
5. Keep on adding to the checklist.

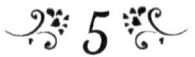

Give A Gift To Yourself - Mental, Physical, Social, And Spiritual Happiness

Everything has been created twice, once on a mental plain and once on a physical plain. – Bob Proctor

Be Good To Yourself

Being hurt doesn't mean that you will punish yourself. Making a mistake doesn't mean that you'll end up getting it more messy. Having failed once doesn't mean that you'll never succeed. All of this shows that you're moving a step ahead in transforming yourself better. So, you've to be good with yourself. You've to be at peace with yourself. You need to be kind, soft-spoken, and forgiving at the same time. You need to have patience to see things becoming better. If you want to see the beauty of the rainbow, first try to enjoy the rain. Feel like the clouds are showering their blessings upon you.

The Key To Happiness

"The more you praise and celebrate your life, the more there is in life to celebrate.' – Oprah Winfrey

It was my 14th birthday. I had fallen in the school playground and hurt my knee the previous day, and it was still paining. But when everyone wished me and gave me beautiful gifts, I forgot all about the pain! Do you remember how thrilled and special you used to feel on birthdays and occasions like Diwali, when people would give you gifts? In fact, why childhood? Gifts always make us happy, no matter what age we are.

We always plan and give a lot of thought to gifts that we give to our beloved ones. We want our gift to be the best. Perhaps it is to see them smile, maybe it is to see their eyes sparkle when they open the gift. But think about it – aren't you your own best friend? Have you ever thought about giving yourself a gift? About making yourself feel special? Life has made us so busy and responsible that we are always thinking of others.

But now it's time to think of yourself too. Now it's time to make yourself happy. In fact, pregnancy is the right time to give yourself "a gift". Ask yourself if you had the time to choose a gift for yourself, what would you choose? Would you choose accessories, fitness equipment, books, clothing or perhaps a spa package? There are unlimited options available! Basically, you will be thinking of things that would make you happy.

The best gift you can give to yourself is *"the key to happiness"*. Yes! Happiness is what you want. No matter how your day was and what all struggles you've had in your life, you just want to be happy at any cost. You want to feel the satisfaction of being happy before going to bed in a grim mood.

You need to find your own key to happiness. You need to identify what makes you happy. What keeps you in a cheerful mood? Is it a cup of coffee or just pampering yourself and taking a break from work? Sit in silence for some time during the day and you'll figure out what your heart says. Let's do it now.

Mental Wellbeing And Happiness

"Going into a pregnancy is a really challenging time for a woman, because it's forever-changing, both mentally and physically." — Brooke Burke

The first pregnancy can make anyone scared, but it's a beautiful journey. I am sure you would also have a lot of questions bombarding your mind about delivery, health issues, the recent changes, etc. But nothing comes easy. We can prepare our mind to get the best result. Being mentally fit plays a crucial role in everyone's life, especially in the expectant mother. Because if the mother feels stressed, then it affects the child anyhow. A healthy and calm mind is always better to tackle things.

How can the mental health of a mother be better?

1. **Meditation:** This is a helpful tool to make the mind calm. You can meditate for at least 10 minutes a day to declutter your mind. If you're new to meditation, you can try guided as well as individual meditation. You should start practicing it twice daily.

2. **Practicing self-love:** Have you read the book by Louise Hay on self-love? If not, you must read it to practice mirror self-love exercise. If you're happy from within, it directly reflects on your face. The foetus will also get positive vibes. Make yourself a priority at least one hour in a day and do what you love. Give time to yourself and do what makes you feel excited about it.

3. **Engage in positive self-talk:** We all know how our body changes during pregnancy. We need to keep our mind in a right frame for such things. You need to understand that there is a life growing inside you. This change is temporary and you will be back in shape once the baby is delivered. So, don't worry. Just try to accept the way you look. You should talk with yourself in the same positive way that you want to hear from other people. Have respect towards your body changes and appreciate it.

4. **Speak your heart out:** Mood swings are common during the pregnancy journey. It happens due to a lot of hormonal changes. You might feel different emotions like happiness, sadness, excitement and joyfulness, etc. at the same time. You feel like you want to go out one moment and the next moment you want to just take a rest. It's important for the expecting mother to express her feelings with her husband and the family. Without sharing, they might not understand what all pregnancy changes you're going through. Sharing not only helps the mom-to-be unburden herself but it also helps others to know what she is going through better.

5. **Engage yourself with other moms-to-be:** This is the best phase to make new friends and take the advice

and the suggestions. You should start interacting with other moms-to-be. You can plan out exercises, get-togethers, etc. to cheer yourself up.

6. **Make the environment positive:** You can create a peaceful environment at home by surrounding yourself with plants, some soft music playing in the background, perhaps some wind chimes, and so on.

7. **Take proper sleep:** A short nap never harms. It recharges our body and makes the mind calm.

It's up to you what you enjoy the most. You need to find your own stress buster in life. Different people like different things such as reading, writing, singing, cooking, photography, travelling etc. These will help you to stay mentally fit during your pregnancy.

What You Shouldn't Do

1. Don't engage in any kind of negative self-talk.
2. Don't demotivate yourself.
3. Don't overthink.
4. Don't read or listen to bad news.

Happiness Through Physical Fitness

This is another thing that plays an important role during the pregnancy. Being physically fit is extremely important as it helps you to prevent swelling, gaining excess weight, and other health complications.

1. **Walk the talk:** Walking is extremely important during the pregnancy phases. As you gain weight slowly, it's advisable that you walk a little slow but not fast.

2. **Sleep:** Make sure you have adequate sleep. Apart from sleeping at night, don't feel ashamed to lie down during the day if you feel sleepy.

3. **Yoga:** You can't do all the yoga poses in the pregnancy but there are a few asanas that you can do depending on the trimester. For example in your last trimester, you can prepare yourself for labour with asanas like the cat and camel pose, butterfly pose, Utkatasana, etc. Refer to Lara Dutta's prenatal yoga link on YouTube.

What You Shouldn't Do

- Don't stand for long periods of time.
- Sit immediately if you're feeling low
- Do household chores to stay active physically but don't overdo.
- Don't overdo vigorous exercise or that which has sudden jerks
- Don't put too much pressure on the feet during exercise.

Social Happiness

Social interaction helps us to rejuvenate and exploring out so many new things. In pregnancy, we feel exhausted but we also feel like we want to know what's happening in the outside world. So, take out sometime to socialize too.

1. **Learn a new skill:** Get yourself involved in some new skill where you can interact with others.

2. **Attend antenatal classes:** Before the baby is delivered, it's better to make ourselves aware about antenatal classes. These classes include exercise depending on the pregnancy trimester, lamaze, breastfeeding, and the delivery.

3. **Make an expecting moms group**: You can start a group of expecting moms. You can get names while visiting the doctor, from Facebook groups, and so on.

4. **Arrange get-together with "would-be parents":** You will find a lot of comfort in such get-togethers where both would-be parents will have the same topic to talk about.

What You Shouldn't Do?

1. Don't surround yourself with negative people.

2. Don't travel much

3. Don't pressurize yourself to go out all the time.

Happiness Through Spiritual Wellbeing

"I believe the choice to become a mother is the choice to become one of the greatest spiritual teachers there is." — Oprah Winfrey

This is one of my favourite ways to destress myself. One should be a little spiritual when it comes to maintaining good mental health. It is perfectly fine if you are not a spiritual person but there are a few things that can help you stay calm.

1. **Meditate:** it's advisable to meditate twice a day. We're already going through a lot of pregnancy challenges, so we need to calm our mind.

2. **Do chanting:** If you enjoy chanting, you can perform that too at your convenient time and place. Om chanting is the most powerful mantra to make our nerves calm.

3. **Write/speak affirmations:** Affirmations are always practiced in the present tense. You can read all the affirmations as mentioned in Chapter 3 to divert your mind to positive side.

4. **Thank you note to the universe:** You can thank the universe for blessing you with positive vibes. Universe has a lot for you, just try to appreciate it everytime.

5. **Visualization:** You can also visualize the day when the baby is delivered in the outer world. You can make anything happened if you visualize anything with the positive feeling and believing that yes, you can do it. Many women visualize of having a normal delivery in the labour room.

What You Shouldn't Do?

Spirituality does not mean believing in everything and it would come true. You should set some realistic goal to get the best out of it. It has nothing to do with the superstitious, the feeling of fear, depression, etc. You have to wear yellow on certain days otherwise something bad will happen, etc. is not spirituality. That is superstition. Spiritual health comes from spending time talking with God so we look at life through eyes of faith.

Books Recommendations:
- The Mind Game by Devika Das
- I love Myself by Vandana Sehgal

Key Takeways:

1. Self-priority is must.
2. Mental Wellness : To have a mental clarity to lead a healthy pregnancy.
3. Physical Wellness: stay active by maintian a proper well-balanced diet.
4. Social Wellness: be excited always for something and try to learn from others.
5. Spiritual Wellness: plays an important role in connecting with oneself.

I want you to write down how have you planned wellness for yourself? Write down everything that comes to your mind.

Hospital Bag Checklist

There are an unlimited number of things that we need on the baby's arrival. Let's make the hospital bag checklist for all the necessary things you will need when you go to deliver the baby. Make sure that you have it ready by the 37th week of the pregnancy.

For Baby

- Diaper bag
- Rompers (minimum 5 to 6)
- 3-6 vests
- Reusable nappies
- Baby jhabla
- 3 pajamas
- 1 warm blanket
- 2 bedsheets
- 3 bibs
- 3 pairs of mittens
- 3 pairs of socks and caps
- Cotton hankies that have been washed and softened
- 2 Baby towels
- Diapers (new born)

- Swaddle blankets (2 nos)
- Quick dry sheet
- Baby wipes

For Expecting Mothers

- Nursing bra
- Nursing pads
- 2 sets of tee and pajamas
- Disposable panties
- Sanitary pads

You can check out a few gifting set options available for the newborn:

- Mee Mee gift set for newborn
- Himalaya newborn gift set

You can check out more good brand options like **Mom & me, Sebamed,** and **Mammaearth,** etc.

Note: The list goes on but I have mentioned a few necessary "must-have" items in the hospital diaper bag for the baby, and for the mother.

- Kindly buy according to the weather
- Always keep the stock extra in advance
- Always go for a patch test before trying any cream, lotion, or oil on a baby's skin
- Buy only cotton clothes that are comfortable to the skin
- Don't use any harsh products on baby's skin

- Don't buy unnecessary items and clothes because in the first two years, as the baby grows, the size keeps on changing.
- Don't go for the brand, but for the quality. Always check ingredients before buying.

How Can You Prepare Your Baby's Room

In the USA, where the gender of the baby is revealed, the parents can plan and design it accordingly depending on the color choices, the interiors, book shelf, toys corner, etc.

But In India too, we can plan out a few things in advance for the arrival of the baby like wardrobe, toys, bookshelf, baby cot, rocker, stroller, and so many things. It needs a lot of planning and the discussion with the experienced parent who can guide in the best possible way. There's nothing to worry as nowadays everything is available online and you can shop from different websites like Amazon, Firstcry, Hopscotch, and many more just after the arrival of the baby too. You shouldn't buy many toys beforehand, because you will need them as the baby grows. With one-day deliveries nowadays, it is always better to buy as you need.

Baby Skincare Products

A baby's skin is too soft and products with harsh chemical can damage the skin. It is advised to consult the pediatrician to check what to use. You can check out products with natural or organic ingredients. If you stock beforehand, you may not be able to use. So, have patience. Just try to make the baby comfortable in first few months.

Key Takeaways:

1. Keep the checklist handy by the 37th week.
2. Be a little prepared in advance.
3. Just feel the positive vibes of the upcoming newborn.

Finally, The Day Arrives: Natural Birth Or C-Section?

"A new baby is like the beginning of all things – wonder, hope, a dream of possibilities." – Eda Leshan

The trimesters of pregnancy are ending now. They were full of mixed feelings where a woman goes through several hormonal changes and emotions, mood swings, the nervousness of being pregnant, the excitement for the day of the baby's arrival, etc.

The 40 weeks of pregnancy play a crucial role in the baby's development in a mother's womb. Each day is precious for achieving the desired milestones. The pregnancy time is full of nausea, heartburn, swelling, gaining weight, exercise, proper a healthy diet, and what not?

The Three Very Important Stages You Must Know About

1. Water Bag breaking
2. A bloody mucus discharge
3. Labor Pain Contraction

Delivery

I remember the day, at the end of the 7th month, when my doctor told me and my husband that the baby's weight is less compared to what it should be. It frightened us and we didn't know what to do. I am grateful for my MIL (mother-in-law) who prepared healthy meals for me and took care of my diet. She forced me to have more protein intake so that the baby could gain weight. By god's grace, when we got the next ultrasound done after a few days, the baby had gained another kilo. We breathed deeply after hearing this.

But now all that is in the past and the time has come when the delivery can happen anytime. In my case, my 38th week was going on. It was Friday, 8th Feb 2019. I had my breakfast a little early and winding up the kitchen tasks, I was getting ready to go to the park for a walk. Suddenly, my water bag broke down, and I was terrified. I changed into my pajamas almost three times and then went to my MIL. She understood the time has come. She asked me to keep my bag and the diaper bag separately. I explained to my husband about the situation and we rushed quickly to the hospital, keeping in mind that we would probably return soon.

My first thought at that time was, "OMG! I forgot to go to the parlor too." My bad luck, it was me who was delaying it. When my gynaecologist came to check on me, she told me the cervix was open around half cm and they couldn't allow us to get back home in such a situation.

I was admitted by 3 pm after my husband did all the formalities. Our heart was dying to see the face of a beautiful soul soon. The doctor decided to induce me. But the pain was not as much as it was supposed to be after getting a lot of high-level doses of injections. It was 9 pm when our doctor finally asked us to wait for one hour more and if the pain was not there, the team would go for a c-section because the head of the baby wasn't in the right position and was not attempting to come out. The doctor instructed us clearly that it could be risky for the baby if we waited for more than an hour.

We did not have much time to decide. The pain was supposed to come in the lower back but it was in the thigh area. After some time, having a discussion with the family members, we all agreed for a C-section. Everything went well and it was 11:07 pm in the operation theatre when I got a tear of joy after hearing her crying. That *"first-cry"* from my bundle of joy will remain in my heart forever.

It's not like that I didn't prepare myself for normal delivery. There are many unforseen circumstances once you are in the labour stage. Any mother who dreams of having a normal delivery, prepares themselves mentally and physically by performing some required exercises. But you never know what could happen at the last moment like blood pressure issues, the baby not supporting, the pain may not be bearable for some or there may be less amniotic fluid, etc. It all depends on the situation. Kindly don't be disheartened. What matters the most is "healthy baby" and the mother to be safe.

C-Section Vs Normal Delivery

"Turn your wounds into wisdom." – Oprah Winfrey

Cesarean or C-section delivery has become an 'epidemic' in India. Although the overall rate of cesarean deliveries in India is around 17% of the total deliveries, rates have risen rapidly over the last ten years from 8.5% in 2005–06 to 17.2% in 2015.

First, let us understand what it is.

What Is C-Section Delivery?

It's a surgical process that takes around 45 minutes. The baby is out within 10-15minutes. The doctor makes an incision through your abdomen and uterus to remove your baby.

The vast majority of C-sections are performed while the mother is awake, and she usually receives either an epidural or a spinal block to numb the lower half of the body. The surgery itself won't hurt because of the painkillers—although you may feel pressure during your C-section and a tugging sensation when the baby is pulled out.

There are stitches on your lower abdomen that you need to take care of properly. The doctor suggests ointment and proper oiling for the same and that has to be maintained until a mother recovers.

What is a Normal Delivery?

Also known as natural birth and vaginal delivery, in a "normal" delivery, the mother doesn't have to go for any surgical procedure. But she can take or may be given an epidural during the process. It's a little lengthy process almost for around 12-15 hours depending on how much the cervix has dilated.

Myths And Facts Of The Two Main Types Of Delivery

So, now after knowing about both the deliveries, let's throw some light on this via sharing a few common myths. Each delivery style has its pros and cons.

MYTH #1: Vaginal delivery is more painful than a C-section

Truth: Yes! A vaginal birth may leave mom with some pain in the perineum — the area between the vagina and anus. But a mother with vaginal delivery recovers a little earlier than compared to the C-section delivery mothers.

Myth #2: A mother cannot have a vaginal birth after a cesarean.

Truth: No! It's not true. I know one of my friends who has gone for vaginal birth after a cesarean delivery for her first baby. All you have to do is to prepare your mind and the body accordingly for the same. It requires consistency and the regularity of deep breathing exercises.

Myth #3: You can't breastfeed after a C-section.

Truth: This is not true. C-section moms breastfeed their babies just as moms who deliver babies naturally. A mother should put an effort in making skin-to-skin contact with the baby and getting emotionally attached. She can breastfeed her baby with the right breastfeeding position.

Myth 4: Having a C-section means you can't get postpartum depression.

Truth: Postpartum depression has nothing to do with the mode of delivery. It's an alternative lifestyle that a new mother has to accept and live this way. Postpartum depression can be handled well with the support of the family members.

Myth #5: C-section deliveries are more expensive than natural ones.

Truth: This is mostly true. However, it depends on which hospital you choose. Vaginal delivery happens at a less rate in government hospitals whereas it's about 10-15% higher in private hospitals. You can consult your doctor regarding this. But you must know what's the difference between a C-section and normal delivery before you choose.

Sometimes, though, as I mentioned earlier, the choice doesn't lie in your hands. There may come a situation during vaginal delivery that compels the doctor to go in for a C-section. Sometimes, on the other hand, you are totally prepared for a C-section but contractions are quick and easy and you have a natural delivery.

You know best how your body reacts. It depends on a mother's intuition and a doctor's experience what type of delivery would be best. A few can't bear the pain of three hours whereas a few stayed in pain for 24 hours to have a natural birth.

Key takeaways:

1. Don't hesitate to go for C-section if need be.

2. Preparing for labour is under you but you can't control the unforeseen situations.

3. It doesn't matter how you deliver the baby - C-section or the vaginal delivery. But the important thing is baby should be healthy and mother should be safe.

4. Just be excited to welcome the newborn in your life.

Conclusion - The Beautiful New Journey Ahead

"God speaks in the silence of the heart." - Mother Teresa

Cheers! Now you are a mom. Here's what the renowned yogi and author, Sadguru, has to say on motherhood: "The beauty of motherhood is not in reproduction, the beauty of motherhood is in inclusion. It's not because your mother reproduced you, that's not why mother is precious. Because in many ways she saw you as a part of herself, it's because of that. Suppose your mother delivered you and never bothered about you, she will be your first enemy. The willingness to include another life is a part of yourself. It is that beauty that we are trying to celebrate on Mother's Day."

I felt overwhelmed when my baby arrived into this world. After a while, the baby met her father and the grandparents, and it thrilled them with a lot of emotions. I had tears of joy when I first saw my little princess. Aww! She looked just like me. How the soul has grown properly inside the womb and has come out properly with a healthy body. All the difficulties of pregnancy and the mood swings, etc., is more than worth it when you see your baby for the first time.

The Highs And Lows Of Pregnancy

Now that your pregnancy has come full term, let's look back and see what were the best and worst things about it.

What're the best things about pregnancy?

- No Periods!! For me, that was the bestest thing ever.
- Expect a lot of pampering. Live like a queen during these days!
- Cravings. Icecreams, pickles, sweet, sour – eat to your heart's content and enjoy every bit of it.
- A lot of shopping. Do I Need to say more? This is one of the best forms of therapy in some ways!
- Unlimited attention. Take advantage of this.
- Relax, read books, do whatever you want. Want a lemonade? Just say it and someone will get it. Enjoy this time.

What's the worst part about being pregnant?

- Mood swings
- Tiredness, feeling low
- Weight gain
- Swelling
- Breathing Issues

The Gender Debate

I always heard the statement, "Blessed are the ones whose first child is a daughter". I never believed in this because I am also a first-child to my parents, but I always imagined having an elder brother who could guide me to certain things. But I was wrong. I believed in the statement only when my first kid was a daughter.

Yes! It's rightly said by someone that it's not about the gender of the baby. But both are equally important and have their role in a parent's life. It's not about the boy or girl every time, but it's about a child who should be born healthy. We all are aware of how our mind behaves when we talk about genders. Over 70% want their first child as a boy. I am not criticizing anyone who thinks that way but want to emphasize that gender doesn't mean anything – having a healthy child is what is most important.

Here, my primary motive to convey this message. Let us understand it via an example. In the USA, they reveal the gender of the baby after three months. And soon-to-be-parents feel blessed to have a baby and celebrate a gender reveal with fanfare no matter what gender it is. But, in India, this is not the case. Gender revelation has been banned because not all Indian parents think the same way. There are a few parents who appreciate and welcome the first girl child. Nowadays, we know and see how girls are growing and excelling in every area of life. They are not less than boys, and stand equally.

I appreciate such parents and feel grateful for the kids who have such parents.

Preparing For The Postpartum

If you are a working mother, or raising the baby by yourself, there are things that you should decide or should have decided about the next phase. For instance – How are you going to look after the baby while you're at work? How to express your milk if need be? What is postpartum depression and how to deal with it. (More about postpartum depression has been given in a later chapter.)

WORKING MOM GUILT

This is small dedication to all working moms contributed by Dr. Abinaya Vijayakumar, Motherhood Empowerment Coach, Author of International No. 1 BestSeller, *Omg! I Am A Mom Now*, and a mother of a 2-year-old son.

Every Monday morning has a hasty and running-on-toes start and mine was not an exclusion.

I have pledged myself earlier at least a thousand times that I will start to my workplace well in advance so that I start my week with a calm and relaxed state of mind but I must admit that I have failed all thousand times

Today was one such day. Once I settled my son with his books after giving bath and feeding him, I had exactly two mins for me to go from "Dull-face-messy-hair-night-dress" look to "fresh-face-neat-hair-professional" look...

I must say I was really quick that I have done it in 1 minute 30 seconds and was rushing downstairs to start from home. I stopped for a while only to see how my kid was positioned so that he doesn't cry seeing me get out of house.

He was surrounded by a pile of his favorite books with one of them open in his hand. He was sitting in the hall telling aloud the names of birds and animals from the book though there was no one who is listening to him.

- I felt guilty for not being able to sit down with him.

- I felt guilty for not playing with him.

- I felt guilty for leaving him alone.

- I felt guilty for being a working mom.

- I felt weak.

- I felt defeated as a mom.

All these emotions flashed by in a matter of seconds. I felt sinking down with guilt. I am not exaggerating. Ask any working mom, she would have experienced or is experiencing the same emotions every day.

I gathered up my courage to reassure myself that

- I am working because I #love what I do.

- I am working because I have my #career and #goals to achieve.

- I am working because I want my son to look up to me as an #inspiration.

- I am working because I teach what #selfdetermination really means.

- I am working to provide a better #future to my kid.

(P.S: To all Moms: Never keep the first reason as kid's future; have courage to say/feel that your goals matter too)

Mom's Guilt is something which can never be escaped but can be reassured. Reassurance and Family Support is very essential in overcoming this.

Rediscover Yourself With The Baby

Here is the personal experience of Rommal Surana, Child And Adolescent Counselor, Founder and Director at Nanhagyan Foundation and a mother of an 8-year-old son.

The word "MOTHER" means something different until you become a mother. The moment you get to know about a baby in the womb - your motherhood journey starts. After that, a woman doesn't think first for herself but for her child. Pregnancy is not always easy. Many women go through physical and emotional roller coaster rides. Yet the essence and presence of the child in her womb gives her contentment and divine happiness. When I got the confirmation about my pregnancy, my world and the people around me changed within a second. Suddenly everyone started caring a

nd pampering me in a manner that I never experienced. I started enjoying the phase. My friend suggested a few practices that would help my baby to develop not only physically but emotionally and mentally. I couldn't understand how my baby will understand complex things

My friend is a Garbha Sanskar Trainer. She advised me some yoga poses to be practiced, diet to be followed. Above all she taught me how to bless food, medicines, water before consuming them. She also shared what needs to be read, mantras to be chanted, which type of music to listen to, how to sleep, what speed needs to be maintained while walking and working, how to talk to the child and respond to all vibes.

I asked her how all these things going to help. She explained to me the first three months of the child are crucial as brain development has started. There are 5 lopes in our brain which represent our five senses. As a mother whatever you experience will be absorbed by child neurons to create its neural pathways. This is a time when innate potentials are developing. As a mother, if you are able to nurture it, this will reflect in your child.

She also added once the child is born the environment also plays an important role. Whatever a child learns is called acquired knowledge. Both Innate potential and Acquired knowledge complete the child's personality. The innate potential is the base of the child's personality in its formative years.

I did follow her. For a month, in one of my antenatal-scan sonography, there was a challenge. As per that sonography, there was a certain reading of brain development that was high. My gynecologist said we need to wait till the fifth month scan to confirm whether I could proceed with this child or not. In those few months, I practiced gratitude. I wrote the gratitude journal. I believed strongly that my child is safe and did affirmation.

I remembered my friend's words, what I experience will affect my child. I was confident and there was no doubt or question during that phase. While doing so, I became optimistic, spiritual (not religious), creative, and developed patience. I was not so before this. I rediscovered myself. I became a better version of myself in this phase.

In my fifth month scan, things were normal. My baby was healthy. I was sure that I will get this news. This made my belief more strong in "What you think, that you become"

Key Takeaways:

1. Just enjoy your pregnancy and make memories.
2. Ask for the help from family members etc.
3. Don't pressurize yourself too much.

PART 2
Cherish The Motherhood

Motherhood is wanting the best for others and not expecting anything in return. - Sri Ravi Shankar

9

Postpartum Blues: How To Handle Postpartum Depression And The Weight Challenge

"I received a great deal of treatment, but I knew in myself that actually what I needed was space and time to adapt to all the different roles that had come my way. I knew I could do it, but I needed people to be patient and give me the space to do it." - Princess Diana

We all are aware that the term "Depression" means a serious medical illness. It negatively affects how we respond to the situation and involves a lot of issues like loss of interest, and losing appetite, etc. It causes a feeling of sadness for a long period if untreated well. But are we aware of "postpartum depression (PPD)"? Postpartum means the time after childbirth. PPD mostly occurs in a new mother just after giving childbirth.

Having a newborn can be exciting, but it is stressful too. No matter how much you're excited at the moment about laughing and bonding with the baby, he or she demands a lot of attention. Considering the sleep deprivation, extra responsibilities, back pain, and mood swings, etc., new mothers are mostly on roller coaster rides. They forget to give some time to themselves, which develops the risk of postpartum depression if not treated well.

There are a few days when a mother cannot cope up with the pressure of handling the newborn. There is a weakness in her she cannot manage. A new mother might not feel as normal as she feels otherwise. She might feel irritable because of the breastfeeding issues or the pressure caused by the family or any relatives, etc.

Some mothers also faces issues like insomnia, sleep deprivation, disorientation, forgetfulness, pain, etc. She may lose her confidence as well because of the excess weight gained just after the delivery. She needs someone to listen to her but most often the advice and attention of everyone is focused on the baby which drives her towards postpartum depression.

What Are The Ways To Overcome The Low Feeling

- Exercise
- Make time to rest
- Practice meditation, do deep breathing
- Examine your breastfeeding – talk to a lactation consultant
- Confront your fears
- Maintain a healthy diet
- Take help from others

This mild low feeling can go on for a long time if not treated well and develop into full-fledged PPD. It becomes the duty of a mother too not to hide anything from her husband/family members and vice versa. A husband/family member plays the best role here, where they can take care of the baby while the mother is sleeping. So, she can sleep peacefully and wake up fresh.

Postpartum Depression

"I thought postpartum depression meant you were sobbing every single day and incapable of looking after a child. But there are different shades of it and depths of it, which is why I think it's so important for women to talk about. It was a trying time. I felt like a failure." - Gwyneth Paltrow

The most common form of depression in women is PPD. It is a mood disorder that occurs after the birth of a child. It certainly does not mean that a mother is not happy to deliver a baby, but pregnancy causes a lot of biological, physical and emotional changes in the mother, and in some these changes bring about PPD.

They feel extreme sadness, anxiety, and exhaustion that may make it difficult for them to complete daily care activities for themselves or for others. Disorders like such only cause self-harm, lack of self-care and difficulty in managing the day to day activities in personal purview.

What Causes Postpartum Depression?

- Constant sleep deprivation can lead to physical discomfort and exhaustion, which can contribute to the symptoms of postpartum depression.

- Drop in the levels of hormones in a woman's body leading to chemical changes in her brain that may trigger mood swings.

- Many new mothers do not get to rest after delivery, which is much needed to fully recover from giving birth.

- A lot of physical changes in the body.

Expert Interview

Here's the interview with expert, Priyank Joshi, one of the top Mental Health bloggers, Founder of Sanity Daily and a mother of 8 years old girl.

Author Radhika: How do new moms identify that they're going through PPD?

Priyanka: Although the most ignored aspect of motherhood, PPD is very common in new moms. Sudden changes in body, daily routine, and overall quality of life, lead to a lot of mental distress in women, which is hard to explain sometimes.

Most often women are criticized for feeling in a certain manner, as the symptoms include anger, frustration, irritability, mixed emotions of guilt, shame and hopelessness.

All these emotions make one confused and it becomes hard for other family members to understand her mindset, ultimately leading to more chaos. If these kinds of thoughts and sadness persist for a long time, one must consult her doctor or seek consultation to understand her thoughts. Ignoring this for a long time will surely hamper the beautiful journey of motherhood.

Author Radhika: How can a family be supportive during this difficult time?

Priyanka: Family members should contribute, help, and support new moms in making her feel comfortable, making her life a little easy with all the possible resources for at least the first three months, right after the baby arrives. This is known as the settling time and when a new mom gets enough support, rest and care, she heals faster from the body changes, weight issues and a lot of hormonal imbalance she has faced in the past few months.

Honestly, this hardly happens in our Indian families and the burden of taking care of the baby, house, and the elder child or children, if the woman already has an elder baby, all falls on the mother. All this then becomes quite a challenging task to deal with, all at once. We need more awareness on PPD, hence more conversations are needed.

Author Radhika: Is it temporary or permanent?

Priyanka: Most of the time it is temporary but in many cases when the symptoms go untreated and ignored, it starts hampering the mood and physical health aspects of the moms. Plus, unsupportive family environment also has a lot to do with it, when the mom herself fails to understand why she is unhappy when everything is so perfect around her, she feels guilty for having such feelings. But it is ok to feel this way, we are humans too.

Author Radhika: Can new moms really come out of this?

Priyanka: Yes, new moms can surely come out of it, if they start preparing for the baby mentally. It is not the financial and family aspect one should think about all the time, it is also the mental health status of the parents on the family way. It is crucial that they are in alignment with their physical and mental health; women should understand their capacity and body needs. She must plan for support beforehand and if she is surrounded with unsupportive in-laws or other family members, she should have her clear boundary set beforehand.

Author Radhika: What are the ways to deal with PPD?

Priyanka: It is important to address PPD, but this is possible only when the woman is aware of it. So talking about it is important, awareness is crucial, as untreated PPD may last even longer.

1) Understand your own self and if you feel that you are not being your true self for the past two to four months, speak out.

2) Seek counselling. It is ok if you cannot visit a doctor or a counsellor in person, you can seek online counselling too.

3) Self-Care. Just because you are a mom now, don't take away the very essence of womanhood out of you. You still deserve all the love and care, as much as you newborn child needs; you cannot pour love from an empty heart. So start filling it with love, care, compassion, kindness, forgiveness for yourself first.

4) Practice self-affirmations and smile.

Author Radhika: How does anxiety, mental illness and depression affect the health of a new mom?

Priyanka: Any mental illness can have a tiring effect on new moms and lead to a lot of confusion and chaos, family members would call it a temporary change in the routine, some will call it hormonal changes, mood swings, but you always know what is happening there inside you.

Nourishing your mental health begins with you, so try to understand and acknowledge your feelings. No matter how hard it is, it will go away when you own them and start working on them. Anxiety and depression can hit anyone at any point of life, but once it is there, it is important to understand that you need care and attention. At the very least, you need to identify the triggers for yourself and develop a few coping skills. Breathing works miraculously for many individuals, reading or listening to shlokas and other religious scriptures have a lot of calming effects too. Identify what works for you and practice it regularly.

Mental health is a part of you and even if you have a condition like PPD or any other illness, it is not YOU, it is a part of you. It can be treated, help is always there, you just need to take command of your life and let nothing come in between you and your newborn. Enjoy your motherhood and have a healthy life.

As per WHO (World Health Organization), globally about 10% of pregnant women and 13% of women who have just given birth experience a maternal mental health disorder, primarily depression.

7 Possible reasons which could lead to maternal mental illness

1. Lack of support
2. Handling things on her own
3. Giving up a high-performance career
4. Hormonal changes
5. Financial constraints
6. Unrealistic needs to be a perfect Mom
7. Unhealthy relationship environment

You can refer to Priyanka's website https://sanitydaily.com for more articles related to mental health.

My Personal Experience

I remember the early days of my motherhood when I wasn't able to cope up with the pressure of being a new mom. Although I didn't know anything, everyone expected that being a mom, I would understand the kid better. But I didn't know why baby was crying; was she hungry, feeling cold, hot, or looking for some comfort? I was fed up of her crying tone. I wasn't able to sleep properly in the night and some days that led me to stay in a sad mood. I felt like I am not a good daughter-in-law, wife, or a mother, who is not able to help the family. But later on, I realized that my priorities are changing now. I remember a normal conversation with Priyanka and she helped me to improve on my thinking pattern. I did a few things as suggested by Priyanka and started feeling better in a few days and improved my relationship with my daughter too. So, once I felt better with myself, taking care of the baby became my first priority as everyone would have wanted. You must never feel shy to talk about your personal problem with the expert. They might help you in a better way to understand things.

The Weight Challenge

How do we get back to our pre-pregnancy shape, weight and fitness? This is important not only from the beauty aspect but in helping us be fit to bring up our child and also to boost much needed confidence.

Here is an Interview with Shweta Patel, internationally certified Weight Loss Coach, Diet Planner, Postnatal Ayurvedic Diet and Nutrition Consultant, Phd researcher and the mother of two girls - a 3-year-old and a 3-month-old. You can reach her via email: shweta.pjbp@gmail.com

Author Radhika: May we know a little about what you do? And how do you help a new mom?

Shweta: I am a Phd researcher, clinical researcher, internationally certified weight loss coach, diet planner, yoga expert, and mother of two little girls. I worked over postnatal mental and physical fitness of thousands of new mothers. I help new moms to lose weight naturally without any fad diets and intensive exercises, so that they can lead a healthy and happy life.

Author Radhika: As we know, you help mothers of kids aged between 0 to 4 years in reducing their pregnancy weight. So, what's the first step towards it?

Shweta: The first step towards the start of the weight loss journey is to understand your body's needs and make up your mind accordingly. Mindset plays a very important role in every single activity.

Author Radhika: What to eat if the mother is craving for more? How can one deal with it?

Shweta: It's ok to eat more but it's not ok to eat anything and everything without knowing its effect on your body. If a mother is feeling hungry, she can choose healthy food options like fruits, smoothies, homemade juices, salads and nuts, etc., rather than opting for ready-to-eat and processed food. You can have fruits like apple, guava, papaya, orange and all seasonal and local fruits. Juices like carrot, orange, spinach, cucumber etc. One can make smoothies with the combination of seasonal fruits and vegetables too.

Author Radhika: How can we ensure that we're taking a properly balanced diet?

Shweta: A balanced diet must have a good portion of protein, carbohydrates and fats. If one is taking all three in the proper amount then you are on a good diet.

Author Radhika: After how many months of delivery should a new mom diet to shed the weight?

Shweta: One should at least take a rest of 60 days to let the body recover fully in both the cases of normal or cesarean delivery. Your body itself will give you signals if you are ok to work on your fitness or not.

Author Radhika: What are the things that a new mom shouldn't ignore?

Shweta: Very important things a mom shouldn't ignore are her health and her self-care. A woman goes through immense stress during delivery. The whole body gets involved in the process. So it is very important to take care of yourself. Ask for help as much as you need. Take a good amount of rest and once you are ready, kickstart your fitness journey.

Author Radhika: Do you provide a proper diet plan or suggest exercise to shed the weight?

Shweta: Yes I focus more on a holistic way of weight loss without affecting the health of a new mom. My focus is more towards diet followed by simple and easy-to-do physical activities. A mother who has put on 20 kgs weight after pregnancy can safely reduce it with some modifications in eating routine. For example she can follow 5 meals a day eating plan and distribute meals into small portions. Start your day with warm water/cumin water/ginger water/fennel water/fenugreek water and after 1-2 hours have high fiber and high protein breakfast as per your liking. Have one seasonal fruits in midday which can be followed by lunch, evening snack and dinner. Make sure you eat less in dinner and have more vegetables in your meals. The gap should be 30-60 min before bedtime. You can choose salads and soups as a filler.

Let The Adventure Begin...

"Travelling in the company of those we love is home in motion." – Leigh Hunt

The following is an excerpt from the book, *Heartbeat: A Journey to Motherhood*, written by Monali Kakoty, a mother of 5-year-pld girl.

Traveling and exploring places make life all the more beautiful and give it a whole new purpose. Besides being an excellent way of learning and acclimatizing your baby, traveling is a great way to rejuvenate yourself. However, often the words "baby" and "travel" simply do not seem to get along. If you are someone who has always loved going to places and are now in a dilemma, starting to get disheartened, and constantly thinking about the impediments of traveling with a baby, please do not be!

Turning Things Around

With careful planning by understanding your baby's preferences and circadian rhythm well, you can certainly create a smooth experience. Interestingly, we traveled more after the birth of our baby than we had in the first three years of our marital life. We took about eight road trips in three years. On her second birthday, we went on a road trip to Agra and visited the Taj Mahal. Surprisingly, she retained the architectural pattern of the Taj Mahal in her mind way too clearly than we ever thought.

Research, Prepare, and Plan

But yes, we planned precisely for every trip and for each day of the journeys. Many children have motion sickness, and they tend to throw up; my daughter had this tendency too. Gradually, we figured out the triggers and took precautions to

avoid her discomfort. And we coordinated the time of travel with her nap timings. We chose destinations where we would not have to travel for more than seven hours a day. We took stops whenever required. We could and would simply pick up everything that we assumed to be required at any point and put it into our car. Road journeys were congenial, and they elated us every time. We avoided traveling during months when the temperatures are extreme to make the transition smooth for our baby and prevent her from falling ill. While working out our travel itinerary, we spent a lot of time researching hotels in terms of their degree of child-friendliness. You can also book a suite room with a kitchen if you want to prepare food yourself, especially for your baby. We prepared an extensive list of baby items. We carried many extra pairs of clothes, shoes, diapers, wet wipes, and such other items. Toilet seat/pot is another essential item once your baby is toilet trained. You can also take your stroller or baby carrier, whatever you use daily. It is also advisable to carry first aid for the baby and keeping a few basic medicines handy for illnesses, such as fever, and upset stomach. Trust me, electrolytes are a huge blessing while traveling with a baby. We would also prepare a detailed list of the food items that our toddler ate—fruits, Cerelac, biscuits, and such other items. Apart from these, we would give her milk, plain rice, and butter roti during meals.

Stay Positive and Keep Your Calm.

There might be times during a trip when things do not turn out the way you expect or the way you want it to. In such moments, do not get disheartened or regret your decision; keep your calm and figure out the best alternative. Work out a solution to your problem. Do not let trivial things ruin your vacation. Driving your own car saves a lot of money. We avoided long weekends and holidays to avoid the tourist crowd. Every three to four months, we would locate a new destination to set forth. It is one of the best gifts you can give to your children and, of course, yourself.

Customize your Holiday

You need not restrict yourself from traveling after your little one arrives. You only need to identify what suits you best and carve out a detailed plan for smooth execution. Even if you have rarely been on a holiday with your family before, I urge you to go for one. You will be truly overwhelmed. The more you travel, the richer you are. Most importantly, a family that travels together stays together!

10
Lessons Learned In My Motherhood Journey

"Only a mother can truly understand the feelings and emotions of another mother". – Radhika

Five Lessons Of Motherhood

There are an unlimited number of lessons that I have learned in these three years of the motherhood journey. I'm sure, there're many, many more to explore but here are a few which I would like to highlight and share with other "moms-to-be" and "already a mother".

1. Be A Responsible Mother

OMG! Responsibility. Such a heavy word. Isn't it? You already had so many responsibilities as a woman, daughter-in-law, and wife, etc. but now as a mother too. Being a mother is not a part-time job but the entire life you're on this planet, even after your kids are married and having their kids. A mother's job never ends.

The first responsibility of a new mother is to take care of her child in every aspect of life. Kids demand attention in everything like physical, mental, social, and spiritual growth and wellbeing. The first 1000 days play a crucial role in the child's development. The father and other family members also play an equal role in the child's upbringing. But, a mother is the first and the last one who has to be responsible for the same.

2. Patience is Tough But Necessary

This is one of the most important traits that a mother must have or build up. Any parent would love to see and do their kids the best possible way. It fills their heart with infinite happiness when they see their kids achieving new milestones every single day. But they often forget that a "slow and steady one wins the race". A child can only achieve something that is within his/her capabilities. We can't force them to achieve beyond it. For example, my kid started walking when she was 9 months old whereas other kids in my surroundings started walking by the age of 1 plus, etc. I thought, now what's next? When is she going to speak? All new mother think of such milestones. When is my kid going to recognize things? When will my child's teeth come out?

But every kid takes his or her own time, which we must appreciate as parents. We need to keep patience and should go with the flow. Every milestone will be achieved in its time and depending on the kid's growth rate.

Similarly, as the child grows, you will need to have patience when your baby no longer listens to you, when you are tired but the baby doesn't want to eat, when you have been trying to make your baby sleep without success for almost an hour. These are the times when you will feel like shouting at someone but mom, be patience, take deep breaths...this too will pass. Keep these things as memories because when the kids grow up, you will look back with love at these frustrating moments.

3. Spending Quality Time is Important

Kids don't demand anything from their parents but what they expect is "quality time". It depicts the time you allot to your kids. It might be listening to them, or playing with them. Mostly, it happens when a father or a mother comes back home in the evening from work. A hug is enough to express how much they missed each other during the day.

Don't feel guilty about the time you spend away from the child because you and your child both need you to be fresh and calm. Unless you get some time on your own, doing work that you love, this won't happen. But, whenever you are with your child, concentrate on him or her, give your child your full attention. Teach her things while playing, tell him stories.

This is much better than being 24 hours with your child and getting frustrated or cranky because of lack of sleep, or looking at the mobile all the time you are there. Even if you are working from home, keep work separate.

4. A Mother is a Multi-Tasker

You never know how strong you're until you're in the situation. Once you enter motherhood, managing multiple tasks comes automatically. You will suddenly become superwoman, and you will soon be cooking, folding laundry, cleaning the living room all at the same time while the baby sleeps. You will check your social media or attend to phone calls while in the toilet.

The priority of a mother is "to take care of her kid" over anything. It comes naturally when you see your baby crying and you realize they need more attention than anything else.

5. Trust Your Maternal Instincts

God gifts this trait to every woman as soon as she becomes a mother. A mother's instinct is damn strong and can never go wrong. A child is always in a mother's thoughts. She knows what's best for him/her before anyone could figure it out. A mother needs to feel proud of herself. I feel blessed when after becoming a mother, my gut instinct always turns out to be correct. It makes me feel more confident. It becomes stronger with time and experiences.

So, if your baby is crying and everyone is trying to play and make her happy, if you know that she is sleepy, just tell everyone to stop and take her away to sleep. Sometimes, a baby may be quiet but you feel something is wrong, take her to the doctor and tell what you feel.

So, Mumma! Don't feel you are incapable or that you don't know anything. You're blessed with everything you need. You have supermom powers now!

Five Things You Need To Stop Doing To Be A Happy Mom

1. Stop Doubting Yourself

We all understand that you're new to your motherhood journey. But, trust the journey of motherhood and have faith in god. God has already given you the power to be a supermom and raise a super kid. You just need to wear the crown and walk like a queen. A mother puts in all the effort while raising her kids and that's appreciated.

2. Stop Comparison

Each child is unique and has a set of qualities. So, won't each mother too be unique? Every mother has her own style of raising her kids. No one knows better than a mother how to deal with her kids, what they want, etc. It is not necessary that you bring up your child exactly the way your friend is bringing up their child. Don't think "Oh, she has bought this new learning toy for her child, I should also buy it. I think this is why my child is not speaking properly till now." If you start comparing things and milestones, there won't be any end to it. Just do things the way you want to, and have confidence on your judgement.

3. Let it Go

People will always make a statement whether you're doing your best or not. They always have something to say. A few people don't want to see you and your kid growing well, they feel jealous. But let this not affect your inner voice of a mother. It all depends on you how you respond to it. You can always take suggestions from others but your heart knows the best for your child. There is no point in arguing or fighting. Do you agree? You can practice meditation to learn the art of letting it go. It'll make you feel calm and more confident. Let your child also know, their mother is the strongest.

4. Stop Feeling Lonely

A mother becomes over-possessive when it is about her kids. But don't let this make you feel arrogant or misunderstood by others. Don't be restricted to the home, kids, and household responsibilities. Starting to socialize with other mothers is a great way to learn from each other's experiences. Keep sometime for your partner too. Sit and have a coffee or go out together for at least 30 mins every evening just the two of you. This is very important.

5. Stop Worrying And Start Living

One must understand that it's your life. Stop pleasing others now. You need to set "me-time" and do what you love the most. You need to set your priorities accordingly but Your priority is you. Make a list of the things you always wanted to do. Set up your day well to keep things organized. Give at least 30 mins to you and something you love doing every day.

So, Mumma! Don't stop loving yourself. Do what makes you "to be a Happy Mom".

Happy Hormones-Happy Mumma

Hormones are the chemicals that are produced by glands present in the body. It affects our body in many ways like it affects our mood, lifestyle, and relationships, etc.

A new mother has to deal with many things like breastfeeding, recovering, and taking care of the baby. She might get frustrated in between following all the chaos. It's equally important to keep your hormones happy while dealing with every task and not pressurizing too much on herself.

There are four types of hormones that make us happy. If we focus on these well, we'll not feel sad or dull. Let's take a look at those hormones which can keep a mother or anyone happy.

1. Dopamine

This hormone is related to the brain reward system. Anything that makes you happy from inside and outside activates dopamine. For example, a little change in your environment, a change in lifestyle, adopting healthy eating habits, etc. A mother can create a happy environment around her baby and that slight change will make her feel happy too.

2. Oxytocin

It is known as the "love hormone". It is activated by the relations that we maintain with our kids and the spouse etc. For example, during breastfeeding, a mother feels happy that her child is taking breastfeed. It sends a signal to her mind and activates oxytocin which helps a mother to produce more milk naturally. Keep some time for your husband or partner too.

3. Serotonin

This hormone is more related to our eating habits. We should eat rich foods like omega-3, nuts, ghee, and lentils to ensure healthy levels of serotonin hormones. Don't go for unhealthy products but add more protein and iron-rich foods to your diet to enhance your mood. A new mother should take care of her diet well to have enough energy to take care of herself and the baby.

4. Endorphins

It is known to reduce stress and pain. A new mother can do this by meditating, journaling, socializing, etc. These activities help her to boost her self-esteem. You can try laughing more, spending some quality time with yourself, healing yourself, etc. to ensure healthy levels of endorphins.

So, Mumma! What're you waiting for? You know the rules of the game now. Learn to play it well and you will have a happy and healthy child, a loving spouse, and a happy you!

Magical Motherhood

"I realized when you look at your mother, you are looking at the purest love you will ever know." – Mitch Albom

The moment I wake up in the morning, the first glance I take is of the face of my beautiful princess. The moment makes me feel lazy to get up, and I want to keep cuddling and giving her more hugs. Omg! She behaves like me as I too used to sleep only by the fragrance of my mother who would be lying just beside me.

I recall all those moments as we were growing up when my mother tried to wake me and my brother up. But our father was always by our side and asked her to let us sleep for some more time. The same is happening with my daughter now. Kids are so lucky in this case. Childhood is when kids were carefree, stress-free, no workload, etc. That is the best time of our life. Once we grow up, we tend to live with our daily routine, meeting deadlines, stress, overthinking, planning, etc. My two-year-old toddler never fails to entertain us except the days when she is not feeling well. She keeps on doing such activities just to make us laugh and ensures that we're responding to her. She makes everyone sit together, eat together, dance together and play together like ring-a-ring- roses where everyone moves around in a circle and she does it so seriously.

There are times when we try to match her latest photos with our childhood pics. This brings back the old good memories. Along with that, my in-laws also share their childhood experiences and we spend quality or family time all together.

I want to capture such moments and get them framed in my heart forever or by just clicking a picture. Not only me and my husband, but the grandparents are also reliving their beloved moments again. Kids are truly God's blessings. "The way they approach us, the way they find solace in our eyes, the way they make us realize that we're everything to them." She has taken us back into our childhood days.

Especially during the lockdown, we've had the best time spent with the family. And I would like to thank my daughter for entertaining, understanding, co-operating and just being with us. *"The best time in the whole day is the time spent with you. I feel disheartened when I ignore you sometimes because you know, Mumma is overloaded with other work. But don't stop making the moments to cherish forever."*

Here are a few points which I wanted to convey to a new mother. Relax! Feel blessed that you're a mother. BE PROUD.

Tip #1 Make Your Own Rules

We have been programmed from childhood days that we should listen to our elders and obey all the rules but the time has changed now. Parents of today's generation are smarter. Here, I am not comparing the love or care. In fact, our parents did the best in raising us up but now today's parents have their parenting style for raising the kids. They believe in living their life more practically. They believe in doing what they feel is right for them and their kid. They are self decision-makers. Earlier, mostly a mother used to stay with the child at home while the father worked. Now, even offices have crèches and there are so many work-from-home options that mothers have no problems in following their own career. Travel with children has also become easier. There are so many gadgets and apps that help us through every process that life is totally different.

What do you think? Is it necessary to obey all the rules once you enter into motherhood?

Tip #2 Organize But Don't Go Into Panic Mode

Is it important to be organized all the time? Undoubtedly, it helps us in many ways once things are organized well... but hold on! Take a breath. We all know you have so many pending tasks like household chores, decluttering wardrobes, washing clothes, office work, and other new daily assignments. When you have a toddler at home, no matter how hard you try, no matter how much effort you put into keep things organized, your house might always seem messy, your work schedules may be all topsy turvy but yes! It's ok.

Omg! oh no! I just kept everything in its place and it's all messed up again. Oh no! He did potty again, I just cleaned him up. Oh no! The baby is not sleeping. But why? Oh shit! Baby has created all the mess again.

Such things will go on in a mother's mind when she loses her cool. Those who have kids at home can relate to me very well. But oh my God! I am a mother... give me the power.

Let them explore things. Let them create the mess. The home can be organized anytime but their toddler time will never come back. So don't pressurize yourself much and just try to relive the moment again with your little one. Thank God! I am a mother of a happy toddler.

Tip #3 Make The Most Of Occassions

Being a new mother, you will be excited to dress up your kids according to the occasion. But, don't forget yourself meanwhile. Buy a dress of your favourite color and texture that will suit you the best. It'll not only make you happy but boost your self-confidence too. A little self-care shouldn't hurt. Go and get a facial done. Take out your jewellery and look good. Take some good pictures. Believe me, you will feel refreshed by this break for the coming weeks.

Tip #4 Overcome The Feeling Of Being Overwhelmed

How innocent and cute my baby looks. But kids are smarter than us. They know the technique to get their work done quickly, even if it is by crying or showing anger etc. We parents get melted with their innocent actions. Here, I would like to share this advice with new and first-time parents, don't feel overwhelmed and try to solve the problem into parts.

You may need to finish a project on a deadline. Don't get overwhelmed. Change your work timing. Start working very early if you are an early riser. That way you will get at least 1-2 hours of worktime before your regular chores begin and you get a head start. Talk to your client frankly if need be and extend your deadline. Yes, you may not be able to work as much as you want to but it's just a matter of a couple of years. You can work twice as hard after that to make up. Another example is don't get overwhelmed with deciding which school to enroll her in while she is still not a year old. You can find out about schools and look at options but there is not a do-or-die situation here. See things from a different perspective and be chilled about life.

Life has given you a gift. Enjoy every bit. Stop worrying about how clean the house is, stop comparing with your friend who always looks perfect. Just enjoy these precious moments with your child and family that goes away so fast. At the same time, it's your life too and you just live once. Don't completely lose track of yourself, of your inner self.

Hats Off To Mothers

I Love You, Maa

I miss you every single second, maa, starting the moment I became a mother. It's been three years of my motherhood journey, and I realize that I respect you more than ever before. You were always right *Maa banne ke baad hi, Maa ki feelings samaj aati hain*... only after becoming a mother do you understand the feelings of a mother. Now I understand and appreciate each effort you have put in upbringing me and my brother. Not only this, you are a multitasker who manages the house, and maintains the relations with love and kindness. There're so many things I want to imbibe from you. A few are like honesty, patience, selfless attitude, and what not!

Now I realize how difficult it is to become a mother. My roles and responsibilities towards life have been increased. I am sorry if I'm not able to talk to you when you need me. I'm sorry for not visiting you. I miss our chai gossip time. Hahaha!!! I know you don't like chit chatting over a cup of tea. I know it takes a lot of effort and patience to raise a kid in all aspects of life. We today's generation are so busy and a little selfish, that we forget that our parents are also growing. We should spend enough time with them to cherish the moments of life.

Itna sukoon aur kaha milega , jab maa kehti hain "kab aaoge milne beta" (Where will we get such peace in our heart as when our mother says, "When will you come to meet me, child.")

I sometimes wonder how you were able to manage everything so well. Now, from the bottom of my heart, I admire you. I respect you for being the CEO of our home. You made me realize that earning is not everything in life but self-satisfaction is. You taught me, we're nowhere if we don't value our relations. I can list an unlimited number of things I have learnt from you. But I want to ensure that I'll put in my best efforts to walk on the path which you have shown me. The two most important are "value relationships" and "never forget to love yourself".

Kabhi kabhi dil bhatak jata hain Maa

iss ajeeb si duniya mein,

bhag padti hu sabko dekh kar unke piche,

Unki tarah, jinko khud ka hi khayal nahi,

Mana ek pehchan banai hain maine,

Lekin woh pehchan mere apno se toh upper nahi,

tab tumhari sikhayi hui baatein yaad aati hain Maa.

Sometimes this heart gets lost , mother

In this strange world.

I ran after everyone seeing them

To be like them, who doesn't even care of themselves

I agree I have created my own identity

But this identity cannot be above my own beloved ones

And then I remember every word that you taught me, mother.

A token of appreciation to my MIL, a personal experience
I am thankful to my coolest mother-in-law (MIL) who enjoys making fresh food. She showers her love via the food prepared by her for anyone in the family. And I feel blessed the way she has taken care of me, my healthy balanced diet, clothes, and everything related to my pregnancy. She went with me for the doctor's appointment with me and reminded me to take medicines on time. She had a discussion with everyone at home to keep the environment happy. And what not! Who for? Of course for me and the baby. She is a religious lady who listens to chanting of "Hare rama hare krishna" or OM the whole day. We both have so many similarities between us like our clothes fit each other well, and we are both great tea lovers. Hahaha! We can talk for hours over a cup of tea. We perform puja together in the evening and enjoys each other's company a lot. We both feel incomplete without each other. Although I may not be able to do all my responsibilities sometimes, she always blesses me with positive vibes. Her aura is so positive that everyone around her feels blessed to meet her. I am thankful to the god who showered me the true blessings via my MIL. I would like to thank her for being with me during my entire pregnancy journey, and for always making me learn new things. She is always patient with me. Thanks a lot for taking care of the baby in my behalf. Because of you, I am able to enjoy my life. I feel truly blessed to be the daughter-in-law of the Jindal Family.

Sach hi toh kaha hain kisi ne,
Ek ladki ki kismat khulti hain,
shaadi hone ke baad,

Lekin, ek beti ki kismat khuli hain,
Saas ke roop mein maa milne ke baad.

Someone has spoken the truth A girl's luck blooms after her marriage But a daughter's luck blooms When she gets a mother in the form of a mother-in-law

The Qualification Of A Mother

When a woman starts her motherhood journey, a lot of questions are already running through her mind. The queries and worries like how she will handle all those kids' trauma, whether her figure will be the same again, the loss of freedom, etc. She is worried whether she'll be able to deliver a healthy baby or not, whether she'll be able to nurture him well or not, etc. These common questions arise in a woman's mind before planning the baby. But, once the baby is delivered after putting all the efforts of healthy meals, being health conscious and monitoring foetus growth, etc., the bundle of joy makes everything worth it.

Once a child is born, everything's changes. A mother is more concerned for her kids than anything else in the world. Her heart, mind, and soul is involved only in concerning the child.

When a baby is born, they know only the mother by their voice, touch, and smell. A kid doesn't know whether her mother is officially qualified or not. They only know she's my mother and they accept her unconditionally. They look forward to her.

Now let me ask you a question, does a mother need a professional degree to qualify herself as a mother? Isn't she blessed with her instincts to know what's happening with her kid - to know questions like why is he behaving like that?

There is not any more precious gift in the world, then the unconditional love of a mother.

A mother plays many roles in her kid's life depending on the situation. A mother is both sugar and spice at the same time. She knows the best thing to do for her kids. Sometimes she's a teacher, friend, role model, financial controller, CEO of house, the best chef, a doctor, a healer, a decision-maker, a counsellor, a reader and the emotional backbone, etc. You all agree that yes, the list could go endlessly.

I feel sorry for those who don't appreciate the efforts put in by their mother whereas a few are struggling to find their mother's true love. I feel sorry for those who keep on insulting their mothers in front of their friends when she's not able to speak English but they forget she educated them so they can learn to communicate well. I feel sorry for those who take their mother for granted but they don't know God is watching over them.

Today's kids don't have time to spend with their parents but they have time to spend with their friends and on other events. They should understand our parents are also growing old with us.. They'll not be here with us all their life. We all are here for a limited period of time. So, why waste it for something else which is not important to us? Indeed, we should spend it with those whose life is nothing without us. We still have time to say sorry and thank you to our parents. Just remember their hard work and try to appreciate every time you notice it before the time is gone.

The primary motive of this chapter is to convey the message that no mother needs a specific qualification to be with her kids. She's just perfect the way she is. She just needs to be a little understood and respected. You'll see how much her heart is an ocean of love. "Make yourself ready to dive in love with your mother everyday."

Write down all the points that you feel like you need to appreciate with your mother. Just give a call to your mother and speak your heart out.

_____
_____
_____

13

Moms Sharing Their Experiences

"Making a decision to have a child--it's momentous. It is to decide forever to have your heart go walking around outside your body." - Elizabeth Stone

Motherhood is scary. Isn't it? Why do you look confused? Ask yourself.

Let me first ask you whether you have been on a roller coaster ride that has a number of ups and downs, that is sometimes very fast and at other times excruciatingly slow. You remember the feeling you get in your stomach before having a fun ride. Either it's fun for you or it makes you feel scared. But once you're on it, you can't come back. In the same way, motherhood is all about ups and down, the sad and happy phases, etc. One moment you're much excited about some small thing and the next moment you feel lost. You don't know what to do next.

Let's hear what other mothers like you have to say about their journey with their children after becoming a mom. Here's some advice, some words of encouragement, and lots and lots of empathy!

Author Radhika: What advice would you like to give to first-time new parents?

Preeti (mother of a 7-year-old boy and a 2-year-old girl): I would like to suggest a few tips to first- time parents.

Firstly, congratulations on the arrival of your little one; it's a wonderful feeling indeed. We do get nervous, excited, scared, and get extra cautious when we hold our baby in our hands for the first time—yes, this bunch of emotions is called Motherhood.

We tend to ask so many questions and also get showered with so many answers when we are expecting, even before conceiving and also after delivery of the baby. People give suggestions according to their experience. Yes, we must listen to all but do what your heart says. Just go with the flow and try to understand what your baby is demanding at that particular time...

Please don't over pamper your child; let the baby grow at her own pace and you grow with them, too.

We tend to ignore ourselves and give our 100% to our growing baby. It's not right to forget to look after oneself. Take out some time for yourself because you deserve to pamper yourself too.

Author Radhika: How do you feel being a mother of two princesses? Don't you feel like you need a boy too? Kindly share some experience about your motherhood.

Palak (mother of two girls, a 5-year-old and a 3-year-old): Somewhere in my heart, I feel that we humans are very selfish. First we ask God to bless us with a child then if we get fortunate enough we start negotiating with God with our priorities of having a girl child or a boy child. I am not targeting any community or an individual.

In fact I myself was one of the victim of these choices. When I conceived my second baby, thanks to our society, I was looking forward or wanting that I should deliver only a boy child since the first was a female. I was doing every possible thing right from the date of planning till a point when I literally got frustrated in order to reproduce a male child. I then realized what foolishness I am into. Instead of thanking the almighty for the grace he has showered on me, I am kind of disrespecting it.

The only blessing one can give a pregnant woman is to deliver a healthy child and for herself to be healthy. But we really land up doing all disgraceful things. Thanks to my Guruji who made me realize that whether a male or a female all are his children and there is nowhere written that only a boy child or only a female child will be the blessed one. We, the 21st century people, have to overcome this and change these substandard talks. I am not trying to be a feminist neither trying to support any masculinity theories but I am only speaking my heart from my experience.

Radhika: You are blessed with a princess. So, when are you planning for the second one?

Shruti (mother of a 4-year-old girl): Planning a family is a very personal thing whether you are planning to become parents for the first or second time, it is never an easy decision. A lot of things have to be evaluated like: Age, Health, Change in diet, Change in lifestyle and so on. We also have to think about what does your partner think about another baby.

Radhika: How do you feel being a mother of two princesses? Don't you feel like you need a boy

too? Kindly share some experience about your motherhood.

Neetu (mother of two girls, a 9-year-old and a 5-year-old): I feel good that I have two kids, even though they are of the same gender. Yes, sometimes I do feel having a boy also, not in the sense of *'Ladka hona chahiye'*, that a boy is a must; but as having kids of both genders to see and feel their behaviors, and their different ways of growing up.

Rest, I am happy to have girls. Both my daughters are also very different from each other. Watching them is a joy, and we are living our (my hubby's and mine) childhood through them.

Radhika: I understand that being a mother of 3 kids is damn difficult? But how do you see your life with three kids? Are you enjoying your motherhood?

Puja (mother of two girls, a 2.5-year-old and a 8.5-year-old, and a 1.5-year-boy): It is very hectic to manage with three kids but I am doing well with that. My kids are very happy and they really enjoy to play with each other. They get to learn from each other. My elder daughter always says momma I have both a brother and sister. My friends have either brother or sister...this really makes me confident about my decision of having three kids

Radhika: What do you think motherhood is? Are you planning for the second child?

Nikita (mother of a 4-year-old girl): Motherhood is a choice which I make everyday to put someone else's happiness and well-being ahead of my own , to teach the hard lesson, to do the right thing and also to forgive myself over and over again for doing something wrong. Motherhood is messy and challenging and crazy and sleepless and giving and still unbelievably beautiful. It's very special feeling which cannot be replaced by anything. Planning for the second one but not anytime soon.

Radhika: What do you think motherhood is all about? How do you manage work-life balance?

Komal (mother of a 3.5-year-old boy): Motherhood is a selfless love bound with your little one. I try to give equal status to both my personal and professional tasks and reserve time slots as needed for each of them.

Radhika: How do you feel being a new mom?

Khushboo (mother of new born): I'm excited and have mixed emotions. My love, my soul, welcoming new life with wide open arms full of bright future!

Radhika: What do you think motherhood is all about? How do you manage work-life balance?

Ishita (mother of a 4 year-old boy): Motherhood is a exploration of unconditional love and care for your child. It's a term that cannot be described in words. You can easily manage work-life balance by doing what you love the most.

Radhika: Are you enjoying your motherhood? What advice would you give to new moms?

Palki (mother of a 1-year-old girl): I would just say to new moms that listen to all but all babies are different. So, accept only that which your baby accepts easily, be it feeding, sleeping, learning, speaking, crawling, etc. Let your baby do all such activities at his or her own pace. Don't take any load, be happy. Your baby is the best teacher.

Author Radhika: Now that your son has grown up, how do you feel being the mother of two grown-up boys? Did you ever feel like you wanted a girl to make your family complete?

Anu (mother of two boys, 17-years-old and 21-years-old): When my younger son was born, I was totally depressed as I was expecting a girl child. But as time rolled on, I have realised that yes I will be mother of girls too someday. I'm eagerly waiting for the day when my two would-be daughters-in-law will fulfill my dream of becoming a mother of a girl and will make my family complete.

I would love to know, at which stage are you right now? You can email me at radhikajindal21@gmail.com

1. Pregnancy
2. Motherhood

What do you think, which stage is the most difficult one?

The Essence of Motherhood

1. Pregnancy
2. Labour
3. Breastfeeding
4. Motherhood

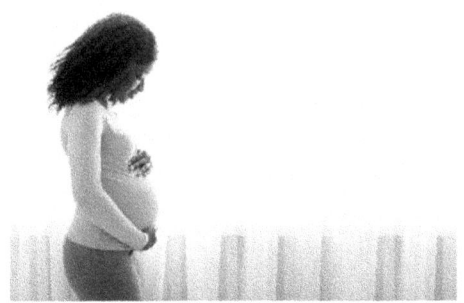

Direct Dil se for on my daughter, Divanshi's 2ⁿᵈ b'day

Dekho dekho 8th feb ki shaam hain
Jaise kal ki hi baat hain
Ek nanhi pari aayi mere ghar
Iss nanhi pari ke janamdin ka dusara saal hain

Aaj mann kar raha hain
Jhum uthu, nachu, gau or khusiyan banau
Jo meri pari ko pasand hain
Jasei dadi ke haath ka badaam ka halwa
Papa ki favorite matar paneer
And hum sabki favorite poori

Uska chehra uske papa jaisa hain
Aur aankhein mumma jaisi
Whi ruthna, hasna or khelna
Aapni zidd se sabka mann jeet lena
Aur phir mithi si muskaan dena

The Essence of Motherhood

Tum aise mann lagati ho sabka
Jaisey gadi ke kante hi nahin hain

Jasey dadi ke saath puja karna,
Dadu ke saath walk par jana,
Bua ke jaane par senti ho jana
Fufu ko smile dena
Bhaiya se secret code mein baat karna
Nanu ke saath gana gana
Nani ke saath dance karna
Mamu se chocolates and gifts lena
Mumma ko kitchen me help karwana
Or papa ke office se aate hi
Pa pa pa karke chipke rehna.

Our best wishes are always with you, our princess.

-Mumma & Papa
(Radhika & Kapil)

References and Books Recommendations

"Books are the quietest and most constant of friends; they are the most accessible and wisest of counselors, and the most patient of teachers."

- Charles W. Eliot

1. Pregnancy Notes, Rujuta Diwekar
2. Passport to a Healthy Pregnancy, Dr. Gita Arjun
3. The Pregnancy handbook for Indian Moms, Dr Vinita Salvi
4. Pregnancy, Nutan pandit
5. What to expect when you're expecting
6. Cooking for Pregnant Women, Sanjeev Kapoor
7. Pregnancy - the complete childbirth book, Nutan Pandit
8. What to expect when you're expecting, Heidi Murkoff
9. Pregnancy Bible, kareena kapoor Khan

Thank You Note

I express my gratitude to you for spending your valuable time with my book. I hope I was successful in adding a bit of value to your life through this work and I would feel more than happy to hear your experience about the book in the form of a review in amazon.in and other social media by tagging me.

I know most people don't like writing a review after reading a book but I recommend you to do that by spending a few seconds for two reasons.

One, your honest reviews could help someone out there who is looking for others' experiences witht the book before buying. Two, it will also help the writers to analyse their work, improve their writing, and provide you with better works in future.

If you wish to share your personal experience with me, you can email me at radhikajindal21@gmail.com.

Connect with me:
Instagram: radhika0001
Facebook: radhikadiary
Website: www.radhikadiary.com

www.ingramcontent.com/pod-product-compliance
Ingram Content Group UK Ltd.
Pitfield, Milton Keynes, MK11 3LW, UK
UKHW022235230426
12048UKWH00018BA/1267